LEARNING TARGETS

LEARNING TARGETS

TARGETS

Helping Students Aim
for Understanding
in Today's Lesson

Connie M. **Moss**
Susan M. **Brookhart**

ASCD Alexandria, VA USA

1703 N. Beauregard St. • Alexandria, VA 22311-1714 USA
Phone: 800-933-2723 or 703-578-9600 • Fax: 703-575-5400
Website: www.ascd.org • E-mail: member@ascd.org
Author guidelines: www.ascd.org/write

Gene R. Carter, *Executive Director;* Ed Milliken, *Chief Program Development Officer;* Carole Hayward, *Publisher;* Genny Ostertag, *Acquisitions Editor;* Julie Houtz, *Director, Book Editing & Production;* Miriam Goldstein, *Editor;* Lindsey Smith, *Senior Graphic Designer;* Mike Kalyan, *Production Manager;* Keith Demmons, *Desktop Publishing Specialist*

Printed in the United States of America. Cover art © 2012 by ASCD. ASCD publications present a variety of viewpoints. The views expressed or implied in this book should not be interpreted as official positions of the Association.

All web links in this book are correct as of the publication date below but may have become inactive or otherwise modified since that time. If you notice a deactivated or changed link, please e-mail books@ascd.org with the words "Link Update" in the subject line. In your message, please specify the web link, the book title, and the page number on which the link appears.

ASCD Member Book, No. FY12-8 (July 2012, PSI+). ASCD Member Books mail to Premium (P), Select (S), and Institutional Plus (I+) members on this schedule: Jan., PSI+; Feb., P; Apr., PSI+; May, P; July, PSI+; Aug., P; Sept., PSI+; Nov., PSI+; Dec., P. Select membership was formerly known as Comprehensive membership.

PAPERBACK ISBN: 978-1-4166-1441-8   ASCD product #112002
Also available as an e-book (see Books in Print for the ISBNs).

Quantity discounts for the paperback edition only: 10–49 copies, 10%; 50+ copies, 15%; for 1,000 or more copies, call 800-933-2723, ext. 5773, or 703-575-5773. For desk copies: member@ascd.org.

Library of Congress Cataloging-in-Publication Data
Moss, Connie M.
  Learning targets : helping students aim for understanding in today's lesson / Connie M. Moss and Susan M. Brookhart.
    p. cm.
  Includes bibliographical references and index.
  ISBN 978-1-4166-1441-8 (pbk. : alk. paper)
  1. Lesson planning. 2. Effective teaching. 3. Academic achievement. 4. School improvement programs. I. Brookhart, Susan M. II. Title.
  LB1027.4.M67 2012
  371.3028—dc23
                        2012003997

22 21 20 19 18   6 7 8 9 10 11 12

We are extremely grateful for our families.

Connie thanks her husband John, parents Rita and Al, sisters Clara and Mary Jo, and uncle Freddie and aunt Rosemarie for their love and understanding. She dedicates her work on this book to Rachael, her beloved daughter and dearest friend.

Sue especially thanks her wonderful husband Frank and daughters Carol and Rachel for their love and support. She dedicates her work on this book to them.

LEARNING TARGETS

Helping Students Aim for Understanding in Today's Lesson

ACKNOWLEDGMENTS

This book would not have been possible if it were not for countless educators across the country whose insights have enriched our lives and inspired us. While they are too numerous to name here, several school districts and educators in Western Pennsylvania deserve special mention.

We are fortunate to continue our decade-long partnership with the Armstrong School District. We extend particular thanks to the members of its leadership team, who have been with us from the beginning: Beverly Long, Shauna Zukowski, and Cheryl Soloski. We owe a debt of gratitude to their principals: Paula Berry, Russell Carson, Michael Cominos, Tom Dinga, James Rummel, Sue Kreidler, Kirk Lorigan, Rox Serraro, and Stephen Shutters. Your critical questions and daily work to help students aim for understanding in today's lesson, and every lesson, expanded our thinking and informed our writing. We also thank Stan Chapp, Michael Glew, Matthew Pawk, and Brad Schrecengost for their support.

We are grateful to the educators of the Norwin School District for their dedication to advancing formative assessment in every classroom. We appreciate their leadership team members William H. Kerr, Tracy A. McNelly, and Mary Anne Hazer for their unwavering support and constant presence in every professional development meeting. We thank their principals and administrators Maggie Zimmer, Edward Federinko, Timothy Kotch, Michael Choby, Joseph Shigle, Robert Suman, Heather Newell, Rosemarie Dvorchak, Brian Henderson, Daryl Clair, M. Joanne Elder, Doreen Harris, and Natalie McCracken for working along with us and their teachers to grow this important initiative. We extend special thanks to a remarkable group of educators, especially Joe Agnew, Carol Borland, Sara Colosimo, Denise Ebbitt, Natalie Janov, Anne Marie Morgante, Larry Paladin, Kelly Sevin, Julia Woitkowiak, and Angelina Yezovich. Your contributions to this work are many. Finally, we gratefully acknowledge the newest members of our Norwin teacher group: Nancy Abramovic, Mandy D'Alesio, Alison McNary, Wendy Melle, Connie Palmer, Scott Patrick, Jared Schultz, Steve Smith, Nicole Stoops, and Lyndsey Young.

Special thanks go to our colleague and dear friend George J. Gabriel and the administrative team of the New Castle Area School District. We especially appreciate your commitment to designing classroom environments that help all children learn and grow. Likewise, we extend our thanks to the district leadership teams from Midwestern Intermediate Unit IV. We specifically thank our dear colleague Cecilia Yauger for her steadfast dedication to making a difference in the lives of children, Virginia Kerr for a lifetime of crucial conversations, and Cathleen Cubelic for her support. We offer heartfelt thanks to the leadership team of the Laurel School District and extend our gratitude to Sandra Hennon and Susan Miller for being shining examples of servant leadership, and to the teachers, psychologists, counselors, and administrators on their leadership team for their commitment to effective instruction and meaningful learning.

We express our appreciation to all of our Duquesne University School of Education family. We extend our deepest gratitude to Launcelot Brown for his leadership and guidance and to our colleagues David Goldbach, Amy Protos, and Susan Bianco for their invaluable contributions. We are privileged to have you in our lives.

Finally, we thank our ASCD editors extraordinaire Miriam Goldstein and Genny Ostertag for their professionalism, good humor, and patience. Thank you for your invaluable feedback and advice. This book would not have been the same without you. We are extremely grateful for your talents and support.

INTRODUCTION: WHY SHOULD WE PURSUE LEARNING TARGETS?

If you ask a teacher, an administrator, and a student the question "How can we raise student achievement?" you'll likely get a variety of answers. Each answer will reveal a personal *theory of action*—that is, the individual's mental map for what to do in a certain situation to produce a desired result. Our personal theories of action determine how we plan, implement, and evaluate our actions. They also guide us in deciding which evidence we accept or reject to help us determine whether or not we achieved what we set out to do.

School districts rarely work with a coherent theory of action on how to raise student achievement. As a result, students, teachers, and administrators are often working at odds, each person doing what he or she believes is best and often misunderstanding one another's intentions and actions.

This book presents a *learning target theory of action* that arose from our research and professional learning partnerships with classrooms, schools, and school districts. These experiences compelled us to write a book explaining the crucial role that learning targets play in student learning and achievement, teacher expertise, and educational leadership.

OUR THEORY OF ACTION IN A NUTSHELL

The most effective teaching and the most meaningful student learning happen when teachers design the right learning target for today's lesson and use it along with their students to aim for and assess understanding.

We believe that improving student learning and achievement happens in the immediacy of an individual lesson (what we call "today's lesson" throughout this book), or it doesn't happen at all. Teachers design the "right" learning target for today's lesson when they consider where the lesson resides in a larger learning trajectory and identify the next steps students must take to move toward the overarching understandings described in standards and unit goals. Individual lessons should amount to something. The right learning target for today's lesson builds on the learning targets from previous lessons in the unit and connects with learning targets in future lessons to advance student understanding of important concepts and skills. That's why we consider important curricular standards *and* the potential learning trajectory as we define the learning target for today's lesson. Our goal is to help our students master a coherent series of learning challenges that will ultimately lead to those standards.

Make no mistake, though: this book is not simply about developing the expertise to design the right target to guide instruction. Our theory of action rests on the crucial distinction that a target becomes a *learning target* only when students use it to aim for understanding throughout today's lesson, and students can aim for a target only when they know what it is. Therefore, we use the term *learning target* to refer to a target that is shared and actively used by *both* halves of the classroom learning team—the teacher and the students.

Teachers share the target with their students by telling, showing, and—most important—engaging students in a performance of understanding, an activity that simultaneously shows students what the target is, develops their understanding of the concepts and skills that make up the target, and produces evidence of their progress toward the target. Together, teachers and students use that evidence to make decisions about further learning.

Learning targets, when shared with and used by both halves of the classroom learning team, are key to creating schools where teaching is effective, students are in charge of their own learning, and administrators lead communities of evidence-based decision makers. As part of a unified theory of action, learning targets compel *all* members of the school to look for and learn from what students are *actually doing* during today's lesson to engage with important and challenging content, develop increased understanding and skills, and produce strong evidence of their learning. In our experience, adopting a learning target theory of action compels schools to reexamine the fundamentals of teaching and learning that positively and powerfully influence student achievement.

WHAT A LEARNING TARGET ISN'T AND IS

A learning target is not an instructional objective. Learning targets differ from instructional objectives in both design and purpose. As the name implies, instructional objectives guide instruction, and we write them from the teacher's point of view. Their purpose is to unify outcomes across a series of related lessons or an entire unit. By design, instructional objectives are too broad to guide what happens in today's lesson.

Learning targets, as their name implies, guide learning. They describe, in language that students understand, the lesson-sized chunk of information, skills, and reasoning processes that students will come to know deeply. We write learning targets from the students' point of view and share them throughout today's lesson so that students can use them to guide their own learning.

Finally, learning targets provide a common focus for the decisions that schools make about what works, what doesn't work, and what could work better. They help educators set challenging goals for what expert teachers and principals should know and be able to do.

HOW WE ORGANIZED OUR BOOK

Our learning target theory of action compels us to pay close attention to what students are *actually doing to learn and achieve during today's lesson*. Throughout the book, we illustrate why gathering evidence about what students are doing, rather than what adults are doing, matters!

The book is organized into nine chapters. Chapter 1 situates learning targets in a theory of action that students, teachers, principals, and central-office administrators can use to unify their efforts to raise student achievement and create a culture of evidence-based, results-oriented practice.

Chapter 2 defines learning targets and provides examples of what they are and are not. The chapter explains where learning targets come from, how they differ from yet are rooted in instructional objectives, and how they propel a formative learning cycle during today's lesson.

Chapter 3 examines what we mean by "sharing" learning targets. It provides strategies for weaving both the learning target and its criteria for success into the fabric of today's lesson. This chapter will also discuss designing a strong performance of understanding (Moss, Brookhart, & Long, 2011b, 2011c; Perkins & Blythe, 1994), which is the most effective way to obtain evidence of student learning.

Chapter 4 underlines the importance of "feeding students forward" during a formative learning cycle to set them up for success. This chapter provides strategies to help students understand how to set mastery goals, produce quality work, and monitor their own learning progress.

Chapter 5 explains the important role that learning targets play in increasing students' capacity to assess their own work and choose effective strategies to monitor and improve that work.

In Chapter 6, we consider how learning targets enable teachers to better communicate exactly what individual students or groups of students should focus on during a differentiated lesson, as well as to customize success criteria and performances of understanding according to diverse student needs.

In Chapter 7, we explain how learning targets promote higher-order thinking through formative assessment and differentiated instruction. Formative assessment and differentiated instruction help make learning targets that involve higher-order thinking accessible to all students. We also demonstrate how learning targets foster goal setting, self-assessment, and self-regulation—processes that influence student learning and achievement.

Chapter 8 looks at the relationships between learning targets and summative assessment and grading. We explain how clearly articulated learning targets help teachers design classroom assessments that summarize achievement over a set of learning targets. The chapter discusses how learning targets connect reportable goals (broader goals for a unit or reporting period) with narrower goals situated in each daily lesson.

Chapter 9 concludes the book with a discussion of how learning targets focus educational leadership practices and collaborative professional development efforts. We explain how learning targets help teachers and administrators align their efforts to improve student learning and achievement. Teachers need to know that there is value in sharing learning targets and success criteria with their students. They also need to know that administrators will look for what students are actually doing during today's lesson to advance their own understanding and recognize the importance and value of teaching this way.

Finally, we include an appendix of action tools that we created during our professional development work with teachers, schools, and school districts to put our theory of action to work across a variety of contexts.

HOW TO USE THIS BOOK

We suggest that you read this book in the order it was written to grasp the fundamental changes in beliefs, reasoning, and practices it promotes. At its core, the book reframes what learning looks like in the classroom and what educators should count as evidence of student achievement. Reading it from beginning to end will help you recognize the relational nature of the chapters to a unified theory of action.

As you begin designing learning targets, sharing them with your students, and using them to guide what you do in your classroom, school, and district, use individual chapters as references to clarify specific points and clear up misconceptions. For example, if you are struggling to grasp the difference between a learning target and an instructional objective, Chapters 1 and 2 clarify this crucial distinction. The theory of action and action points laid out in Chapter 1 combined with Chapters 2 and 3 provide context and practical strategies for reframing learning at the classroom level and explain why the role that students play in their own learning matters. Chapters 6 and 7 deepen understanding of how differentiated instruction and formative assessment combine to promote learning and higher-order thinking for all students. School administrators will find practical ideas throughout the book, but we suggest a close reading of Chapters 1, 2, and 9 to bring coherence to professional learning and school improvement initiatives.

We hope the learning target theory of action and action points in this book lead to courageous conversations. If we truly intend to raise student achievement, then all members of the school—students, teachers, principals, and central-office administrators—must recognize who is achieving and who is not, and hold themselves and others accountable to do something about it.

LEARNING TARGETS:
A THEORY OF ACTION

HOW TO CATCH A MONKEY IN THE WILD: A CAUTIONARY TALE

There are probably many ways to catch a monkey in the wild. One of the most effective is insidious in its simplicity.

The hunter gets a coconut and bores a small, cone-shaped hole in its shell, just large enough to allow a monkey to squeeze its paw inside. The hunter drains the coconut, ties it down, puts a piece of orange inside, and waits. Any monkey that comes by will smell the orange, put its paw inside the coconut to grab the juicy treat, and become trapped in the process. Capturing the monkey doesn't depend on the hunter's prowess, agility, or skill. Rather, it depends on the monkey's tenacious hold on the orange, a stubborn grip that renders it blind to a simple, lifesaving option: opening its paw.

Make no mistake: the hunter doesn't trap the monkey. The monkey's abiding tendency to stick firmly to its decision, ignore evidence to the contrary, and never question its actions is the trap that holds it captive.

THE BELIEFS THAT WE HOLD AND THE BELIEFS THAT HOLD US

The beliefs that we hold also hold us. Our beliefs are the best predictors of our actions in any situation (Schreiber & Moss, 2002). And, like the monkey's death grip on the orange, our beliefs are deeply rooted, often invisible, and highly resistant to change. That's why so many "tried-but-not-true" methods remain alive and well in our classrooms despite clear evidence of their ineffectiveness. Take round-robin reading, for example. This practice has been rightly characterized as one of the most ineffectual practices still used in classrooms. You know the activity: the first student in a row reads the first paragraph from a book, the second student reads the second paragraph, and so on. Round-robin reading has long been declared a "disaster" in terms of listening and meaning-making (Sloan & Latham, 1981), and the reading comprehension it promotes pales in comparison to the effects of silent reading (Hoffman & Rasinski, 2003). So why do teachers still choose it for their students, and why do the principals who observe it in classrooms continue to turn a blind eye?

As our cautionary tale illustrates, it is essential for us to recognize our tendency to hold on to unexamined beliefs and practices. Each of us has our own mental map, a theory of action that directs our behavior in any situation (Argyris & Schön, 1974). What's tricky is that we actually operate under dual theories of action: an *espoused theory* and a *theory in use*. Our espoused theory is what we *say* we believe works in a given situation, whereas our theory in use is what actually guides our day-to-day actions (Argyris & Schön, 1974). For instance, if you ask a teacher what he believes makes assignments meaningful, he might tell you that students should be engaged in authentic tasks. Yet a visit to his classroom might reveal students copying vocabulary definitions from their textbooks. If you want to uncover what someone truly believes about any situation, look for what that person actually *does* in that situation.

Learning involves detecting and eliminating errors (Argyris & Schön, 1978). When something isn't working, our first reaction is to look for a new strategy—a way to fix the problem—that will allow us to hold on to our original beliefs, and to ignore any research or suggestions that go against our beliefs. Argyris and Schön (1974) call this belief-preserving line of reasoning *single-loop learning*.

Deeper levels of learning happen when we uncover what is not working and use that information to call our beliefs into question. When we question our beliefs and hold them up to critical scrutiny, we engage in the belief-altering process of *double-loop learning* (Argyris & Schön, 1974). Double-loop learning is how vibrant organizations change and grow (Argyris & Schön, 1978; Schön, 1983).

When Nobel laureate and astrophysicist Arno Penzias, honored for his discovery of cosmic microwave background radiation, was asked what accounted for his success, he replied, "I went for the jugular question. . . . Change starts with the individual. So the first thing I do each morning is ask myself, 'Why do I strongly believe what I believe?'"

The best way to eliminate the disparity between what we say and what we do and to invite the jugular questions is to forge a unified theory of action, shared across a school or district, that both explains and determines the actions that members take as individuals and as a community.

THE LEARNING TARGET THEORY OF ACTION

In the introduction to this book, we included a "nutshell statement" of our theory of action: *The most effective teaching and the most meaningful student learning happen when teachers design the right learning target for today's lesson and use it along with their students to aim for and assess understanding.* Our theory grew from our continuing research with educators focused on raising student achievement through formative assessment processes (e.g., Brookhart, Moss, & Long, 2009, 2010, 2011; Moss & Brookhart, 2009; Moss, Brookhart, & Long, 2011a, 2011b, 2011c). What we discovered and continue to refine is an understanding of the central role that learning targets play in schools.

Learning targets are student-friendly descriptions—via words, pictures, actions, or some combination of the three—of what you intend students to learn or accomplish in a given lesson. When shared meaningfully, they become actual targets that students can see and direct their efforts toward. They also serve as targets for the adults in the school whose responsibility it is to plan, monitor, assess, and improve the quality of learning opportunities to raise the achievement of *all* students.

When educators share learning targets throughout today's lesson (a subject we discuss further in Chapter 3), they reframe what counts as evidence of expert teaching and meaningful learning. And they engage in double-loop learning to question the merits of their present beliefs and practices.

THE MULTIPLE EFFECTS OF A LEARNING TARGET THEORY OF ACTION

Effects on Teachers

Learning targets drive effective instructional decisions and high-quality teaching. Teaching expertise is not simply a matter of time spent in the classroom. In truth, the novice-versus-veteran debate presents a false dichotomy. Teachers of any age and at any stage of their careers can exhibit expertise. What expert teachers have in common is that they consistently make the on-the-spot decisions that advance student achievement (Hattie, 2002).

Designing and sharing specific learning targets to enhance student achievement in today's lesson requires and continually hones teachers' decision-making expertise. Teachers become better able to

- Plan and implement effective instruction;
- Describe exactly what students will learn, how well they will learn it, and what they will do to demonstrate that learning;
- Use their knowledge of typical and not-so-typical student progress to scaffold increased student understanding;
- Establish teacher look-fors to guide instructional decisions; and
- Translate success criteria into student look-fors that promote the development of assessment-capable students.

Guided by learning targets, teachers partner with their students during a formative learning cycle to gather and apply strong evidence of student learning to raise achievement (Moss & Brookhart, 2009). And they make informed decisions about how and when to differentiate instruction to challenge and engage all students in important and meaningful work.

Effects on Students

When students, guided by look-fors, aim for learning targets during today's lesson, they become engaged and empowered. They are better able to

- Compare where they are with where they need to go;
- Set specific goals for what they will accomplish;
- Choose effective strategies to achieve those goals; and
- Assess and adjust what they are doing to get there as they are doing it.

Students who take ownership of their learning attribute what they do well to decisions that they make and control. These factors not only increase students' ability to assess and regulate their own learning but also boost their motivation to learn as they progressively see themselves as more confident and competent learners.

Effects on Principals

When building principals look for what students are doing to hit learning targets during today's lesson, they improve their leadership practices. They become better able to

- Recognize what does and does not work to promote learning and achievement for all students and groups of students at the classroom level;
- Use up-to-the-minute student performance data to inform decision making; and
- Provide targeted feedback to individual teachers, groups of teachers, and building faculty as a whole.

Guided by learning targets, principals can promote coherence between actions at the classroom level and actions at the school level. They can also better allocate resources to promote student learning and lead professional development efforts in their building.

Effects on Central-Office Administrators

A learning target theory of action also enables central-office administrators to gather up-to-the-minute data about what is working in their classrooms and schools. They become better able to

- Identify key elements that support a districtwide strategy to raise student achievement;
- Communicate the relationship among these elements in an integrated and coherent way; and
- Use strong and cohesive performance data for decision making.

Guided by learning targets, central-office administrators can implement effective strategies to increase student achievement across buildings with different needs and unique characteristics shaped by the students, teachers, administrators, parents, and community members who work together in each building. They can develop and manage human capital to carry out their strategy for improvement, gain district coherence, and make the strategy scalable and sustainable.

Making each lesson meaningful and productive requires collective vigilance. It's not enough to "know" what works. Each day, students suffer the consequences of the mismatch between what we say is important and what actually happens during today's lesson.

THE NINE ACTION POINTS

A learning target theory of action embodies the relationship among essential content, effective instruction, and meaningful learning. The nine action points that follow advance this theory of action and provide context for the ideas and suggestions in this book:

1. Learning targets are the first principle of meaningful learning and effective teaching.

2. Today's lesson should serve a purpose in a longer learning trajectory toward some larger learning goal.

3. It's not a learning target unless both the teacher and the students aim for it during today's lesson.

4. Every lesson needs a performance of understanding to make the learning target for today's lesson crystal clear.

5. Expert teachers partner with their students during a formative learning cycle to make teaching and learning visible and to maximize opportunities to feed students forward.

6. Setting and committing to specific, appropriate, and challenging goals lead to increased student achievement and motivation to learn.

7. Intentionally developing assessment-capable students is a crucial step toward closing the achievement gap.

8. What students are *actually* doing during today's lesson is both the source of and the yardstick for school improvement efforts.

9. Improving the teaching-learning process requires everyone in the school—teachers, students, and administrators—to have specific learning targets and look-fors.

Action Point 1: Learning targets are the first principle of meaningful learning and effective teaching.

The purpose of effective instruction is to promote meaningful learning that raises student achievement. The quality of both teaching and learning is enhanced when teachers and students aim for and reach specific and challenging learning targets.

It's logical, really. To reach a destination, you need to know exactly where you are headed, plan the best route to get there, and monitor your progress along the way. When teachers take the time to plan lessons that focus on essential knowledge and skills and to engage students in critical reasoning processes to learn that content meaningfully, they enhance achievement for all students.

As Figure 1.1 illustrates, where you are headed in the lesson makes all the difference. Defining the lesson's intended destination in terms of a specific, challenging, and appropriate learning target informs both halves of the classroom learning team—teachers and students. Teachers and their students can codirect their energies as they aim for the shared target and track their performance to make adjustments as they go. Defining the right target is the first step and the driving force in this relationship.

1.1 The Role Learning Targets Play in Raising Student Achievement

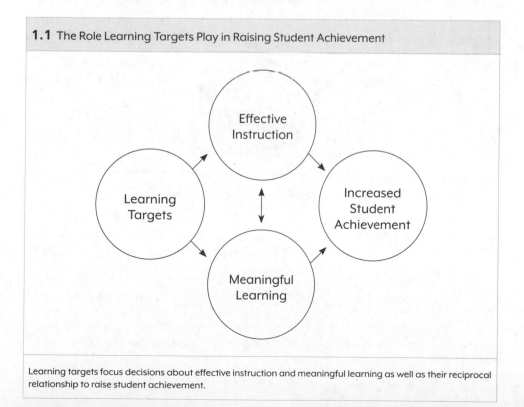

Learning targets focus decisions about effective instruction and meaningful learning as well as their reciprocal relationship to raise student achievement.

A learning target guides everything the teacher does to set students up for success: selecting the essential content, skills, and reasoning processes to be learned; planning and delivering an effective lesson; sharing learning strategies; designing a strong performance of understanding; using effective teacher questioning; providing timely feedback to feed student learning forward; and assessing learning. The combined effect of these actions on student achievement depends on the target's clarity and degree of challenge.

Figure 1.2 shows the elements of effective instruction that require and are strengthened by learning targets. The quality of these elements depends on defining a significant learning target.

1.2 The Central Role of Learning Targets in Effective Teaching

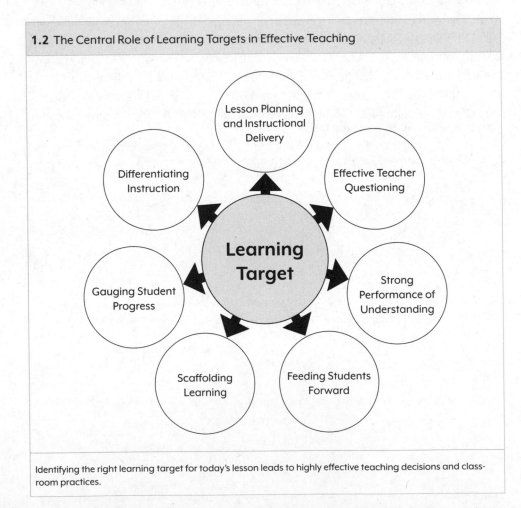

Identifying the right learning target for today's lesson leads to highly effective teaching decisions and classroom practices.

Larry, a high school social studies teacher, explained the effect of learning targets on his instructional decision making:

> Taking the time to define the learning target for today's lesson brings laserlike precision to every decision I make. Once I know exactly where my students will be heading during the lesson, the learning target becomes the scalpel I use to trim and shape the lesson so that the essential content, skills, and reasoning processes take center stage. Now that I know what I want them to achieve, I can evaluate my instructional decisions as I go.

Similarly, meaningful student learning happens when students know their learning target, understand what quality work looks like, and engage in thought-provoking and challenging performances of understanding. These experiences help students deepen their understanding of important content, produce evidence of their learning, and learn to self-assess. When students self-assess, they internalize standards and assume greater responsibility for their own learning (Darling-Hammond et al., 2008). Figure 1.3 (p. 16) shows the elements of meaningful student learning that require and are strengthened by learning targets.

A curriculum director explained the effect that learning targets had on meaningful student learning in her district in this way:

> Not only are we seeing student achievement increase, but the quality of what students are achieving is also increasing. Now that our students understand where they are headed in the lesson, they are more involved in their learning, taking more pride, digging deeper, and persisting.

Action Point 2: Today's lesson should serve a purpose in a longer learning trajectory toward some larger learning goal.

An all-too-common misconception about learning targets is that they are broad statements of what students are going to learn over the course of a week or a unit. A learning target is good for only one lesson, describing the lesson's unique learning intention: why we are asking our students to learn this chunk of content in this way on this day. For example, the purpose of the lesson might be to

- Introduce a new concept or skill (e.g., "Describe the characteristics of the solar system");

1.3 The Central Role of Learning Targets in Meaningful Student Learning

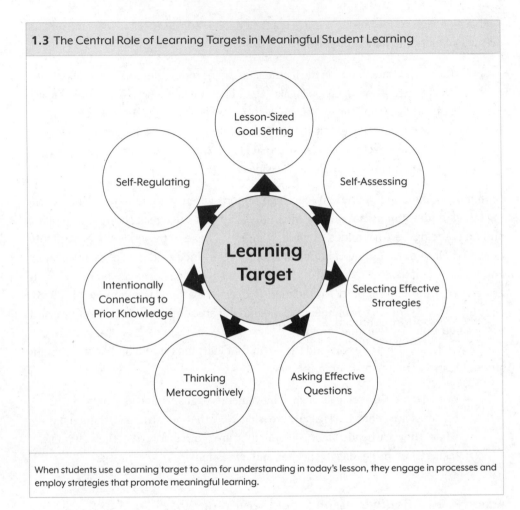

When students use a learning target to aim for understanding in today's lesson, they engage in processes and employ strategies that promote meaningful learning.

- Examine a specific part of a concept or skill (e.g., "Compare and contrast the characteristics of the planets");
- Put learned parts of a process together to form a more sophisticated concept or skill (e.g., "Explain the role of gravity in the workings of the solar system");
- Apply a learned concept in a new context (e.g., "Use 21st century knowledge to critique the ideas of Ptolemy, Aristotle, Copernicus, and Galileo about the solar system");
- Build on a shallow concept to deepen it (e.g., "Demonstrate and explain how the Earth's axial tilt causes the seasons");

- Reteach a concept to clear up points of confusion (e.g., "Sort out and clarify misunderstandings that occur when we apply the terms *revolution* and *rotation* to relative movements of planets and moons");
- Close gaps in understanding (e.g., "Describe how the tilt of the Earth causes the summer season to occur in a specific hemisphere while understanding that the hemisphere tilted toward the sun will experience summer *not* because it is closer to the sun than the other hemisphere"); or
- Extend learning about a concept (e.g., "Describe how asteroids and comets fit into the solar system and the characteristics that distinguish them from one another").

The learning target for today's lesson depends on logical and sequential planning based on long-term and short-term goals and on what students already know and can do. The crucial questions become

- What did students learn in yesterday's lesson?
- How well did they learn it?
- Where are they confused?
- What can they use meaningfully?
- Where is their learning heading in upcoming lessons?

A lesson should never ask students to do more of the same. Each lesson should have a specific purpose—a reason to live. If the adults in the school cannot define and share that purpose, then the blind are leading the blind. If neither half of the learning team—students nor teachers—knows where the learning is headed, then neither one can make informed decisions about how to get there.

Action Point 3: It's not a learning target unless both the teacher and the students aim for it during today's lesson.

When learning targets frame a theory of action for advancing and assessing student achievement, everyone in the classroom understands and aims for the same target. A learning target provides a clear direction for the energy of the classroom learning team and results in meaningful learning and increased student achievement.

Without a learning target, the two halves of the classroom learning team expend their energy in different directions. Figure 1.4 (p. 18) shows what happens when a teacher relies on teacher-centered instructional objectives to guide planning and teaching. The teacher is the only one in the classroom who knows where the lesson is headed and expends a great deal of energy trying to get students to meet the instructional objective. Meanwhile, the students spend the bulk of their energy figuring out how to comply with what the teacher says.

1.4 How Instructional Objectives Work

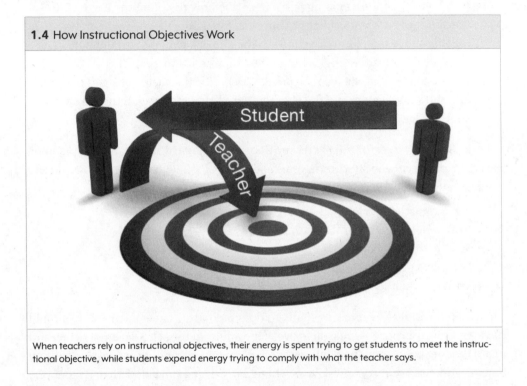

When teachers rely on instructional objectives, their energy is spent trying to get students to meet the instructional objective, while students expend energy trying to comply with what the teacher says.

In contrast, learning targets help teachers and students forge a learning partnership in the classroom. As Figure 1.5 shows, energy converges on hitting the target. Both halves of the classroom learning team know exactly what they are aiming for in today's lesson—what students will come to know and understand, how well they will know it, and how they will provide evidence that they know it.

Action Point 4. Every lesson needs a performance of understanding to make the learning target for today's lesson crystal clear.

Ask yourself, "How do I know what students know?" Knowing what students know and drawing valid conclusions about their developing expertise should be based

1.5 How Learning Targets Work

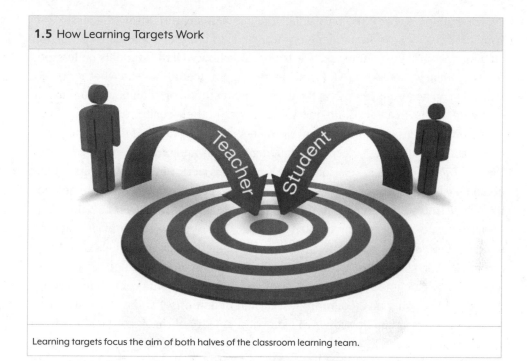

Learning targets focus the aim of both halves of the classroom learning team.

on strong, up-to-the-minute evidence. A performance of understanding—a learning experience that deepens student understanding and produces compelling evidence of where students are in relation to the learning target—provides evidence that both halves of the learning team can use to raise student achievement. Like Cinderella's slipper, this performance is a perfect fit for the learning target and makes the target crystal clear to everyone in the classroom.

We commonly issue a three-part challenge to teachers, building principals, and central-office administrators to highlight the connection among learning targets, a performance of understanding, and data-driven decision making. First, we ask them to observe a lesson *without* consulting the teacher's lesson plan. They must simply observe and describe what students are actually doing during the lesson. Then they answer two questions to evaluate what they observed, based only on what the students actually did during the lesson: (1) Did students deepen their understanding of essential content and skills? and (2) What evidence did the students produce that supports your conclusions about what they knew or were able to do?

For example, what if the only thing students actually did during the lesson was copy vocabulary words and definitions from a textbook, chalkboard, or website like dictionary.com? You wouldn't be able to conclude how well the students understood the vocabulary, would you? The only evidence you would have is whether or not students can accurately copy (in the case of the textbook or chalkboard) or cut and paste the results of an accurate query (in the case of the website).

An effective lesson contains a performance of understanding that requires students to aim for the target, deepen their understanding, and produce evidence of what they know and can do in relation to the target. This performance of understanding could take five minutes or the entire lesson, but every lesson needs one. Remember: it isn't a learning target unless both halves of the learning team see it and aim for it.

In the second part of the challenge, we ask the observer to interview several students before, during, and after the lesson, asking the following questions: "What are you learning in this lesson, and how will you know if you've learned it?" When the lesson doesn't include a performance of understanding, students commonly describe a task ("I'm copying my geography words and definitions") and cite the teacher's assessment to explain how they will know the quality of their work ("My teacher will grade my paper"). If the students aren't required to do a task that deepens their understanding during the lesson, their responses tend to be vague ("geography stuff" or "rivers and oceans"), and their gauge of how well they are doing continues to be the teacher ("We're having a test on this stuff on Friday").

For the third part of our challenge, we ask the observer to interview the teacher using the following questions: "Exactly what were students supposed to learn during this lesson, and how do you know for sure who learned it and how well they learned it, and who didn't learn it and why?" More often than not, the teacher's response begins with "hopefully": "Well, hopefully they got the idea that the circulatory system is responsible for transporting important nutrients throughout the entire body," or "Hopefully students learned that balancing a chemical equation means they are establishing the mathematical relationship between the quantity of reactants and products." When pressed to identify the evidence they used to draw their conclusions about how well the class or specific students learned the content, teachers often refer to upcoming tests ("We'll know for sure when I grade their end-of-unit test"); homework assignments ("Tomorrow we'll go over their homework and get an idea of where we stand"); or a lack of student questions during the lesson ("Believe me, if they didn't get it, they'd let me know about it").

Our three-part challenge reveals the crucial role that learning targets play for all stakeholders. Without a learning target (coupled with a performance of understanding that requires students to use and aim for the target in today's lesson), it's unlikely that teachers, students, and administrators will make informed, evidence-based decisions about student learning. Knowing exactly what students must come to understand in today's lesson and having the opportunity to gather and assess strong evidence of that understanding are essential to raising student achievement both in the short term and over the long haul.

A word of caution: do not conflate the performance of understanding with the learning target. In the tale of Cinderella, the intention (the learning target) was to find Cinderella. Trying on the glass slipper (the performance of understanding) focused the search and provided the evidence. Likewise, the ultimate goal of today's lesson ought to be raising student achievement. To raise student achievement, however, we must ask ourselves, "Achievement of what?" Making decisions about achievement means that we are looking for and weighing evidence of something. The learning target identifies specifically what that "something" is in today's lesson. The learning target answers the question "Achievement of what?" The performance of understanding asks students to "try on" the target during a meaningful learning experience that produces strong evidence of student learning *while* students are learning. A performance of understanding enables both teachers and students to gather information and use it to improve the quality of their work.

Action Point 5. Expert teachers partner with their students during a formative learning cycle to make teaching and learning visible and to maximize opportunities to feed students forward.

Learning targets propel a formative learning cycle in today's lesson. The cycle (illustrated in Figure 1.6, p. 22) begins during the lesson's introduction as the teacher models and explains the learning target and continues as the teacher provides guided practice. Once students understand the concept and skills, the teacher engages them in a performance of understanding, provides formative feedback about the performance, and gives students the opportunity to improve their work. It is this "golden second chance" that makes the difference.

1.6 The Formative Learning Cycle

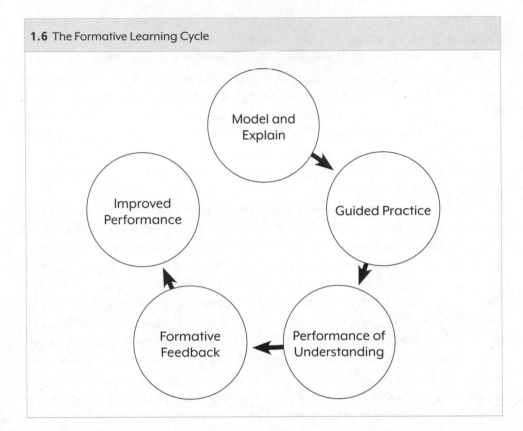

A formative learning cycle embodies the following research-based factors that improve student learning and achievement:

- Learning targets and success criteria;
- A classroom learning team;
- Consistent, targeted feedback that feeds learning forward;
- A built-in chance for students to use feedback to improve their work;
- Goal-setting and goal-getting opportunities that promote self-regulation and self-assessment; and
- The formative assessment process.

A formative learning cycle goes hand in hand with formative assessment, which we define as "an active and intentional learning process that partners the teacher and the students to continuously and systematically gather evidence of learning with the express goal of improving student achievement" (Moss & Brookhart, 2009, p. 6). A formative learning cycle provides opportunities for continual feedback and yields evidence that addresses the three central questions of formative assessment: Where am I going? Where am I now? How can I close the gap between where I am now and where I want to go? (Hattie & Timperley, 2007; Sadler, 1989). The "I" in all three questions stands for the teacher *and* the students.

A formative learning cycle makes teaching and learning visible in ways that raise student achievement (Black & Wiliam, 1998; Hattie, 2009). No one in the lesson is flying blind. The teacher and the students function as copilots; either of them can be the "agent" of the formative learning cycle. The focus is on how the information they gather informs the decisions they make. And even though the teacher will make most of the decisions, the cycle develops students' abilities to make informed decisions that influence their achievement as well (Wiliam, 2010).

Action Point 6. Setting and committing to specific, appropriate, and challenging goals lead to increased student achievement and motivation to learn.

Increases in achievement correlate directly with the degree to which students and teachers set and commit to challenging goals—both distal (long-term) and proximal (short-term).

Think of distal goals as the ultimate destination—where teachers and students are headed over a unit of study. Learning targets subdivide distal goals into lesson-sized proximal goals. These proximal goals become the mile markers we use to measure how well we are doing along the way and to help students recognize that they have what it takes to finish their journey.

Distal and proximal goals serve different but equally important purposes. Students benefit from the motivational pull of long-term goals ("I will be able to use the scientific method to help me solve everyday problems") to increase their interest in tackling short-term goals and to sustain their resolve as they deal with setbacks along the way ("I need to improve the accuracy of my field notes to make sure my observations reflect what is happening in my experiment"). In their turn, proximal goals "provide immediate incentives and guides for performance, whereas distal goals are far too removed in time to effectively mobilize effort or direct what one does in the here and now" (Bandura & Schunk, 1981, p. 587). If a student aims for the lofty, long-term goal of being a better reader and then sets a general proximal goal of "doing my best" during today's lesson, the process will have little effect on the "here and now" or the "ever after." Students need specific short-term goals to aim toward—for example, "Today I will look at words I do not know to see if they contain root words that can help me figure out their meaning."

It is important that goals are set at the appropriate level of challenge. Achievement is an upward-spiraling process: if students do not hit the target in today's lesson, achievement stalls. And if the degree of challenge in tomorrow's lesson does not increase appropriately, achievement plateaus or derails completely.

During instructional planning, expert teachers use specific learning targets to remove distracting items and irrelevant tasks from today's lesson. In doing so, they make it more likely that students will focus on and commit to reaching the goals embedded in the learning target and learn to set their own goals in the process (Locke & Latham, 2002).

Interestingly, Locke and Latham (1990) found that working toward a challenging goal positively affects student achievement regardless of who sets the goal. Still, keep in mind that although teaching students to set goals is important, it is the process of feeding them forward toward an appropriately challenging goal that creates student buy-in. When teachers give feedback to students who have no commitment to reaching the learning target, the feedback packs little punch. Conversely, asking students to set goals without giving them the benefit of teacher feedback packs no learning punch at all (Locke & Latham, 1990).

Feeding students forward helps them consistently succeed, recognize their success, and attribute that success to what *they* do—meaning that an occasional failure or setback will be less likely to dampen student optimism or resolve. Feeding forward also means that students will "set and get" an increasing number of challenging goals.

Action Point 7. Intentionally developing assessment-capable students is a crucial step toward closing the achievement gap.

One of the most effective steps we can take to close the achievement gap is to teach all students how to self-assess and give them plenty of feedback as they are doing so (Hattie, 2009, 2012; Moss et al., 2011c). Assessment-capable students engage in the lesson as active partners who co-construct learning with the teacher. They understand and continually use student *look-fors*—the success criteria for today's lesson—to recognize how well they are doing. When they discover they are not progressing, they ask effective questions. They seek feedback from a variety of reliable sources, including their teacher, their peers, and information resources like rubrics, books, and media. Then they use that feedback to figure out the next steps to take in their learning. During a formative learning cycle, student questioning is taught, valued, and expected as one of the indicators of meaningful learning (Moss & Brookhart, 2009).

Assessment-capable students are resilient, have stick-to-itiveness, learn how to thrive on challenge, and develop a can-do attitude. Each day, they pursue a slightly more challenging learning target and benefit from being fed forward to meet it. They understand that meaningful learning is a deliberate pursuit of increased knowledge and skills that requires successful learning strategies. They also realize that their errors and missteps are important sources of information that they can use to learn about what is working and what is not, and to decide what they should do next.

Assessment-capable students develop in classrooms led by *expert*—not necessarily *experienced*—teachers (Hattie, 2002). Expert teachers consistently make decisions that increase student achievement and motivation to learn. They intentionally help students hone their metacognitive and decision-making skills and provide appropriate degrees of challenge and support to help students master targeted concepts and learn to monitor their own progress.

Action Point 8. What students are *actually* doing during today's lesson is both the source of and the yardstick for school improvement efforts.

Our theory of action supports using what happens in today's lesson to advance and gauge school improvement efforts. After all, that's how kids live their learning—one lesson at a time. A districtwide initiative to raise student achievement should be fueled by data that accurately represent the real-world data model. And the real world of schools happens one day and one lesson at a time.

Summative classroom assessments and standardized tests are macro-level data. They act as wide-angle lenses and provide the big picture of what is happening over time in a classroom, building, or district. These sources of information tell us the general achievements of a specific student or a group of students by subject, time period, grade level, or other grouping.

Looking for what students are *actually* doing during today's lesson is like using a close-up lens. These data yield a detailed view of what happens during a particular lesson in a particular classroom to pinpoint what is working in the lesson—and what is not—for a particular student or group of students.

Schools need both long-term and short-term goals. Graduating a class of self-regulated, assessment-capable, and lifelong learners doesn't just happen because we say it will. It happens when students set specific goals during today's lesson to reach their learning target, select appropriate strategies to help them get there, receive quality feedback that helps them gauge their progress against a set of student look-fors, and then use their new learning to meet the challenges in tomorrow's lesson. The long-term goal gives us something to shoot for, but what's happening in today's lesson makes or breaks our chances for raising student achievement in significant and meaningful ways. A learning target theory of action uses evidence that comes from the classroom to inform our decisions about what it takes to develop expert teachers, accomplished administrators, and schools that produce competent young adults and lifelong learners.

Action Point 9. Improving the teaching-learning process requires everyone in the school—teachers, students, and administrators—to have specific learning targets and look-fors.

Observing isn't the same as seeing. Our own research convinces us that educators do not describe what they see during a classroom observation; rather, *they see what they can describe* (Brookhart et al., 2011; Moss, 2002). For example, a principal who does not understand the characteristics of a performance of understanding can observe 1,000 lessons and never distinguish lessons that have one from lessons that do not. Our theory of action urges students, teachers, principals, and central-office administrators to look for and learn from what effective instruction and meaningful learning look like.

Compare this theory of action with the more traditional use of classroom look-fors. Usually, look-fors are what adults—most often building principals—use to observe teachers and assess their instruction according to a list of "best practices." Unfortunately, no two lists agree on the specific practices they contain and the number of best practices they direct observers to look for. What's more, "best practices" tend to mean different things to different observers. Ask 20 principals what "engaged learning" looks like, and you will get 20 different descriptions. What is most troubling is that traditional lists assume that all "best practices" have the same power to raise student achievement. There are no *neutral* educational practices; they all affect learning for better or worse to some degree. Many so-called best practices exert minimal influence on student learning. If we want to finally close the achievement gap, we should concentrate on advancing practices that make a *significant* difference in student learning and achievement (see, for example, Darling-Hammond et al., 2008; Hattie, 2009).

Here's the bottom line: a list of best-practice look-fors rarely adds up to a cohesive theory of action. All members of the school—students, teachers, principals, and central-office administrators—need to use look-fors. Each person should be assessing his or her success according to a cohesive set of criteria. Each person can claim success when the agreed-upon, research-based actions that they take raise student achievement during today's lesson. With a learning target theory of action, all stakeholders in the learning community know where they are and where they are headed and use strong evidence of student achievement to decide how to close the gap between the two.

LOOKING FORWARD

In Chapter 2, we examine how to design specific learning targets for today's lesson—the first principle of meaningful learning and effective instruction.

2

HOW TO DESIGN LEARNING TARGETS

Many readers may remember being asked to write instructional objectives on the board for students to see. Supervisors checked to see whether your objective was on the board and evaluated you accordingly. The reasoning went that students would do better if they knew the purpose of the lesson and understood the intended outcome.

The reasoning was great; it was the method that was wanting. Consider an instructional objective in teacher language, maybe something like "Students will be able to explain the importance of the cycle of pollination and fertilization as it relates to seed production." It is off-putting at best, because it refers to students in the third person. And it is confusing at worst, because the students probably don't understand what that sentence means. They haven't studied these concepts yet.

Students *do* need to know the purpose of the lesson and understand the target they're aiming for. But most students won't get that from an instructional objective. They *will*, however, get it from a learning target.

MINING THE INSTRUCTIONAL OBJECTIVE: WHAT IS THIS LESSON'S REASON TO LIVE?

Learning targets use words, pictures, actions, or some combination of the three to express to students, in terms the students understand, the content and performance they are aiming for. Your learning target should spring from the instructional objectives that guide a set of lessons in this particular unit of study. Of course, your instructional objective for the lesson should be solid, teachable, assessable, and appropriately derived from curricular goals and state standards.

To plan effective instruction, teachers need to know three things about today's lesson:

- What are the essential knowledge (facts, concepts, and generalizations or principles) and skills (or procedures) for the lesson?
- What is the essential reasoning content for the lesson?
- What is the potential learning trajectory in which the lesson is situated?

If you mine the instructional objective for these three elements, you'll come up with the raw material you'll use to design the learning target. It is not overdramatic to call these ingredients the lesson's "reason to live." If the essential elements of the lesson are trivial, or if they do not advance learning on a trajectory toward more learning, then it is questionable whether this lesson should be taught at all. The whole concept of standards-based instruction assumes that individual lessons, over time, will amount to achievement of a larger standard. Figure 2.1 illustrates this concept and the thinking associated with it.

2.1 Where Does the Lesson Reside in the Potential Learning Trajectory?

Where are my students headed? What specific content (concepts and skills) must be in place to lay the foundation for the next lessons?

What must my students learn during this lesson so they will be prepared to tackle the content and the reasoning processes in the next lesson?

What did my students learn in previous lessons? What can I build on? What should I reteach? What concepts can I enrich or expand? What should my students practice?

The following sections discuss the four steps of designing a learning target.

STEP 1: DEFINE THE ESSENTIAL CONTENT FOR THE LESSON

To define the essential content for the lesson, you need to have a deep understanding of the intended learning. If you find yourself able only to list the facts and concepts that students should know, without placing them into any larger learning picture, you should work on your own understanding before you try to plan instruction.

You also need to have a good idea of what a lesson-sized "chunk" of your instructional objective looks like. What portion or aspect of the instructional objective are you going to work on during today's lesson? All of it? Part of it? If the latter, which part? You can and should communicate longer-range goals to students, but don't lose sight of the fact that students need a learning target for today's lesson.

Once you have a deep understanding of the instructional objective and what aspect or aspects of it you will base your lesson on, ask yourself the following questions:

- What content knowledge does this lesson focus on? Content knowledge should be more than facts; it should also include concepts and generalizations or principles.
- How will this particular lesson add to what students have learned in previous lessons?
- How will this lesson increase students' understanding of the content? Will students develop a more sophisticated understanding of a concept, or will they tackle a brand-new concept?
- What skills does this lesson focus on? *Skills* is a broad term, encompassing abilities like outlining, summarizing, questioning, graphing, diagramming, balancing equations, solving problems, journaling, giving a speech, and using dictionaries and other reference materials.
- Will students learn a new skill, practice one they have yet to master, or apply a highly developed skill to a new context?

STEP 2: DEFINE THE REASONING PROCESSES ESSENTIAL FOR THE LESSON

A taxonomy of thinking skills, like Bloom's Revised Taxonomy (Anderson & Krathwohl, 2001) or Webb's (2002), is helpful here. Ask yourself the following questions:

- What thought-demanding processes will allow my students to build on what they already know and can do?
- What kinds of thinking will promote deep understanding and skill development so that students can analyze, reshape, expand, extrapolate from, apply, and build on what they already know?

STEP 3: DESIGN A STRONG PERFORMANCE OF UNDERSTANDING

A performance of understanding simultaneously serves an instructional purpose (developing student understanding and skills) and a formative assessment purpose (providing compelling evidence of student understanding and skills). So it's important to ask yourself, "What performance of understanding will help my students develop their thinking skills and apply their new knowledge?"

Be careful here. The performance of understanding is not the instructional objective, but it embodies and exemplifies the instructional objective, so it influences the language used in framing the learning target for students. This is a subtle but vital point: one of the most common mistakes teachers make in lesson planning is to confuse learning targets with performances of understanding (Clarke, 2001).

Think of it this way. A performance of understanding provides one of a number of possible ways in which students can learn and produce evidence of what they are learning in today's lesson. Imagine a foreign language class whose learning target is for students to be able to carry on an everyday conversation in the foreign language with same-age peers. Today's performance of understanding has students working in groups, holding conversations that they might have at a friend's birthday party. The performance of understanding could have been a conversation at the ice-skating rink, or in the school parking lot, but it wasn't. There is typically a whole set of performances of understanding that would work for any given instructional objective. Your job is to design a performance that matches the chunk of the instructional objective that is the learning target for today's lesson.

The performance of understanding is what keeps students' heads in the game as they work toward a learning target; from their point of view, what you ask them to *do* becomes inextricably bound to what they intend to *learn*. As the facilitator of student learning, the teacher has the "omniscient" point of view. He or she is able to select performances of understanding and other lesson elements from the larger domain, which includes what learning came before and what will come after. In contrast, students have the "limited" point of view; they are "in" the learning and know only the things they either encounter in the lesson or have prior knowledge of. So for students, doing well on the performance of understanding *is* the goal, at least at that time and in that place. For the teacher, it is only one indicator of learning.

STEP 4: STATE THE LEARNING TARGET

During this step, you describe the lesson-sized chunk of learning for your class as a statement of what the students will learn and do during the lesson. Make sure that this learning target expresses, from the students' point of view, the knowledge and skills they will be using in their performance of understanding.

So far, we have established that developing a learning target follows a thoughtful process of mining your instructional objective for the lesson. The result should be a coherent set: your instructional objective, your students' learning target, and the performance of understanding.

An effective learning target must speak to students, express the essentials of the lesson, and provide students with a rationale for why what you are asking them to do is in fact a performance of understanding. In effect, an effective learning target helps students hop onto the learning trajectory.

Stating a learning target well is a skill in itself: you must state the target in a manner that students will understand, using student-friendly language and relevant illustrations. In the following two sections, we take up each of these in turn.

Use Student-Friendly Language

In the plain English sense, "student-friendly language" means language that students can understand. In practice, the term is often taken to mean using simple words and short sentences. That's a good start, but it doesn't guarantee student understanding. To take a ridiculous example (we love those—people remember them!), consider telling a group of 2nd graders, "We will be able to explain how Hamlet felt about his mother."

Do use simple words and short sentences, but don't stop there. The language of learning targets should enable students to see themselves as the agents of learning. Using the first person works well: targets that start with "we" or "I" communicate to students that they are the ones who will be doing the learning. Clarke (2001) suggests using the phrase "We are learning to . . ." to begin learning targets. Sometimes a set of "I can" statements works, too. You can also take cues from the language your students use in the classroom when they describe their understanding. Figure 2.2 provides some examples of writing learning targets in student language.

2.2 Writing Learning Targets in Student Language		
Guiding Question	**For Younger Students**	**For Older Students**
What will I be able to do when I've finished this lesson?	**I can . . .** • Use question marks.	**I can . . .** • Explain the effect that Ross Perot, a third-party candidate, had on the election of President Bill Clinton.
What idea, topic, or subject is important for me to learn and understand so that I can hit the target?	**To be able to do this, I must learn and understand that . . .** • Question marks come at the end of asking sentences. • An asking sentence usually begins with a word that asks a question, like who, what, when, where, why, and how.	**To be able to do this, I must learn and understand . . .** • The characteristics of a third-party candidate. • The economic conditions in the United States in 1992. • The platform and financial resources of Ross Perot.
What will I do to show that I understand the target, and how well will I have to do it?	**I will show I can do this by . . .** • Changing telling sentences into asking sentences.	**I will show I can do this by . . .** • Writing an essay on the role Ross Perot played in the 1992 election of Bill Clinton that includes three specific effects supported by documented facts from valid and reliable sources.

Use Relevant Illustrations

A strong performance of understanding functions as an illustration of the learning target. From a student's point of view, the performance of understanding implies a learning target that says, "I can do that."

Illustrations or demonstrations that show students as well as tell them about the learning target are powerful. A strong performance of understanding is the most important but not the only way to illustrate a learning target. What makes a particular illustration useful is that it helps focus students on what they are supposed to be learning. Effective ways to illustrate learning targets include

- Showing examples of the kinds of problems that students will learn to solve during the lesson (e.g., $\sqrt{4} + \sqrt{9} = \sqrt{\square}$).
- Drawing a diagram or chart illustrating the kind of thinking that students will learn to do during the lesson (e.g., a Venn diagram or a time line).
- Using a story or scenario known to students (e.g., recent tornadoes in the South).
- Using students' real-life experiences (e.g., shopping).
- Creating an experience for students (e.g., viewing a video clip).
- For certain learning targets, demonstrating the skill itself (e.g., tying your shoes).

Showing examples, using students' real-life experiences, and creating an experience are especially effective ways to illustrate learning targets.

SHOWING EXAMPLES. Sometimes you can communicate a learning target to students simply by rephrasing your instructional objective in words they can understand and adding some examples. This method works well near the end of a group of lessons focused by mastery-type objectives, where the goal is for students to learn a specific skill and its underlying concepts.

For example, in a 3rd grade mathematics class, your instructional objective might be "Students will be able to use place value to compare two whole numbers (as greater than, less than, or equal to each other)." You know that your students are already familiar with the concepts *greater than, less than,* and *equal to,* as well as the symbols for those concepts, and you know that you introduced place value at the beginning of the unit. So today, you transform your instructional objective into a learning target and criteria for success simply by telling and showing:

> Today our learning target is to put numbers in order using the *greater than, less than,* and *equal to* signs and to be able to tell how you use place value to do that. Here are some of the kinds of problems you can solve if you meet your target: 378 □ 387 ; 154 □ 593. Listen for two things as your classmates work the problems on the board: did they talk about place value as a way to solve the problem, and did they put the correct sign in the box? Then ask yourselves the same questions as you work.

Most of the teachers we work with would also write an abbreviated version of this target on the board, such as "Use place value to put numbers in order" and the two example problems.

USE STUDENTS' REAL-LIFE EXPERIENCES. An 8th grade teacher has this instructional objective: "Students will interpret poetry by analyzing the effects of literary devices (e.g., alliteration, metaphor, symbolism, and imagery) on a poem's meaning." This isn't an all-or-nothing objective specifying mastery of specific content; rather, it describes a developing skill that students apply to increasingly complex poems over time. So the learning target comes from the chunk of the instructional objective that the students will see as the short-term focus for today's work.

In this lesson, the teacher is going to work with Edgar Allan Poe's poem "The Bells." She might communicate the learning target by starting with a question: "Think of some different kinds of bells you have heard. Describe the sound of one of them. What does that sound make you think of? How does it make you feel?" After a brief class discussion of these questions, the teacher says,

> Today, our learning target is to be able to describe how Poe thought and felt about different kinds of bells, and to explain how we can figure that out from his poem. We'll know we are successful when we can explain how imagery from the poem creates thoughts and feelings for readers in as much detail as we just explained how real bells conjure up thoughts and feelings in us.

This way of illustrating the learning target doesn't mean that students (or the teacher) lose sight of the essential questions and the big ideas, like "Poetry uses imagery to express meaning, and certain literary techniques are common in poetry because they work with both the sound and the meaning of the words." Using real-life experiences to communicate the learning target engages students' attention and enables them to succeed in the immediate context of the lesson as well as building up, over time, their understanding of the big ideas.

CREATE AN EXPERIENCE. This strategy doesn't work with every kind of learning target, but when it does work, it's powerful and fun. We know of a middle school English teacher who wanted to demonstrate to his students what it meant to be able to use persuasion in a lesson on persuasive writing. He enlisted the help of a colleague and friend in creating an experience for students.

The other teacher knocked on the classroom door at the start of class and came in dressed in shabby pants with holes in them, an old stained flannel shirt with buttons missing, and worn-out work boots. He was lugging a loaded green plastic garbage bag, which seemed to be heavy. He carried it carefully into the classroom and set it down on the floor with a flourish and a pat. He proceeded to talk affectionately to "Ol' Bag," thanking him for being a good buddy and for all the great times they had had together.

Over the course of about five minutes, the skit revealed that the man was down on his luck, needed to leave town, and needed money. Otherwise, by golly, there would be no way he would even consider parting with Ol' Bag. Useful for all sorts of things, was Ol' Bag. A pillow at night, a cushion by day, a place to "put stuff," a friend to talk to . . . By the end of the five minutes, he had succeeded in selling Ol' Bag to a group of students for a dollar. The man left the bag in the classroom, wished everyone farewell, and left with the money (which he eventually returned, of course).

The teacher smiled at his class. "That," he said, "was persuasion. You are going to learn to create writing that can talk people into doing things they might not think they want to do, like buying a bag of old garbage."

PUTTING IT ALL TOGETHER: A 6TH GRADE TEACHER DESIGNS LEARNING TARGETS

Let's walk through an extended example to show how to put all these steps together. Consider a 6th grade teacher who is preparing a mathematics lesson on variability. She starts with the standard, unpacks it down to the objective for one or several lessons, and writes her objective for the lesson. Now she knows what *she* wants students to accomplish during the lesson. Next, she uses the four-step process to express what *students* should aim to accomplish during the lesson.

Common Core State Mathematics Standard 6.SP.1, under the heading *Develop understanding of statistical variability,* reads

> Recognize a statistical question as one that anticipates variability in the data related to the question and accounts for it in the answers. For example, "How old am I?" is not a statistical question, but "How old are the students in my school?" is a statistical question because one anticipates variability in students' ages.

Standard 6.SP.2 reads

> Understand that a set of data collected to answer a statistical question has a distribution which can be described by its center, spread, and overall shape.

To begin to work on these standards, the teacher wants students to develop a basic understanding of the concept of variability (which will be new to most of them) and build on their previous work on graphing as a way to move into the concept. Thinking about her students' learning trajectory in this way, and mindful of the standards toward which the trajectory is leading, the teacher writes these instructional objectives:

- Students will explain how the element of chance leads to variability in a set of data.
- Students will represent variability using a graph.

Figure 2.3 (p. 38) illustrates how the teacher mined these instructional objectives using the four steps we described in this chapter. At each step, she thought about potential learning trajectory considerations, both general (keeping students' learning headed toward the standards) and contextual (keeping in mind what her particular students had done before).

Notice how the teacher thinks about these questions. To identify the essential skills in these objectives, she avoids the temptation to just list the concepts: chance, variability, data set, graph. Of course these are essential elements of the objective! Listing the concepts, however, gives only a surface-level analysis of the content elements. As she thinks about the learning trajectory, the teacher recognizes that the students have already developed some relevant concepts and skills (seeing and understanding patterns, making bar graphs). Other relevant concepts and skills (understanding the nature of chance and its representation as variability in data) will need to be developed.

Similarly, to identify the thinking skills her students will need, the teacher resists the temptation to just pull out mental actions from the objectives: explain and reason, represent and interpret. As she thinks about the learning trajectory, the teacher sees that students have practice with some relevant thinking skills (brainstorming, analysis, cause and effect). Other relevant thinking skills (prediction, especially about everyday occurrences) will need to be developed.

She uses these conclusions to decide that her performance of understanding must give students a chance to use some skills they already have (observing, graphing, and analyzing) to learn new things, namely to develop a mathematical understanding of how chance operates in a data set from everyday life. She then plans her performance of understanding. She will ask students to count the number of chips in a set of chocolate chip cookies and make bar graphs of what they find. Students will

2.3 Defining the Specific Learning Targets for a Lesson in Four Steps

Instructional Objectives for the Lesson

- Students will explain how the element of chance leads to variability in a set of data.
- Students will represent variability using a graph.

Steps	Potential Learning Trajectory Considerations	Elements for the Lesson
Step 1. Define the essential content (concepts and skills) for the lesson.	• My students can create a simple bar graph given a set of data. • My students have a naïve idea about the concept of chance, and this lesson will deepen that understanding. • My students have a solid understanding of how to look for and represent a pattern. • My students already know that chance exists in games like bingo, dice, cards, etc., but do not understand that chance exists naturally in the everyday world.	**Content:** • My students must learn that chance occurs naturally during everyday procedures—like when they make cookies. • My students must learn that chance causes the values in a data set to vary. • My students must learn that variation in data creates a pattern.
Step 2. Define the reasoning processes essential for the lesson.	• My students have little practice with mathematical prediction. • My students have experience with analysis. • My students can build on what they know about cause and effect. • My students know how to brainstorm.	**Reasoning Processes:** • My students must learn to analyze an everyday procedure to recognize the elements of chance embedded in that procedure that might cause a data set to distribute itself randomly.

Steps	Potential Learning Trajectory Considerations	Elements for the Lesson
Step 3. Design a strong performance of understanding that will develop student thinking and understanding and provide compelling evidence of student learning.	• My students can observe and analyze a simple procedure. • My students need to demonstrate an understanding of cause-and-effect reasoning. • My students have practiced brainstorming reasons for common occurrences.	**Performance of Understanding:** • My students must engage in a performance of understanding that simulates naturally occurring elements of chance in ways that require them to observe, graph, analyze, and explain the effect that chance has on data patterns. We will use data on the number of chips in chocolate chip cookies for these purposes.

Step 4. State the learning target.

• We will be able to see a pattern in graphs we make about the number of chips in our cookies, and we will be able to explain what made that pattern.

do this in groups to share the work of breaking up the cookies, counting the chips, and constructing the graphs. The result will be five graphs, one from each group, and they will all be a little different. Students will look at the graphs and discuss their observations. The teacher will lead this discussion by using open-ended questions.

Now the teacher is ready to state the learning target for students:

• We will be able to see a pattern in graphs we make about the number of chips in our cookies, and we will be able to explain what made that pattern.

She will present this target to the students at the beginning of the lesson, refer to the target during students' work, and revisit the target at the end of the lesson. The students can use the target throughout to keep themselves on track, asking questions like

• Am I making a good graph about these chips?
• Can I see a pattern in my graph or in someone else's?
• What does the pattern show?

Notice how different those questions are from typical "good-student" questions like

- Am I doing what the teacher told me to do?
- Am I doing it right?

This process should enable both the teacher and the students to focus their energy on the same learning target, relieving the teacher of the burden of causing learning herself. It requires teachers to take a thoughtful approach to standards and to have deep pedagogical and content knowledge, an appreciation of student learning trajectories, and a respect for multiple perspectives on learning.

Learning targets make the difference, from a student's point of view, between complying with teachers' requests and pursuing their own learning. Students who pursue their own learning demonstrate increased motivation, learn more, and develop stronger metacognitive skills than do students who merely comply with teacher requests. For one thing, they can tell you what they have learned!

LOOKING FORWARD

By now, you should have an understanding of how learning targets work and how to state them, but using learning targets effectively requires two more elements: criteria for success and a plan for sharing the targets and their success criteria with students. In Chapter 3, we discuss these elements in depth.

SHARING LEARNING TARGETS
WITH STUDENTS

Consider two classrooms where students are studying William Shakespeare's *Julius Caesar*. Ms. Thompson begins her lesson by saying,

> Today we will continue reading *Julius Caesar*, pages 462 to 472. Answer the
> questions in the study guide as you read. The first 30 questions focus on facts
> about Shakespeare's early life, and the next 30 outline facts about Julius Caesar.
> To answer questions 60 through 75, you must define the archaic terms from the
> play. Use your dictionaries for this. Remember, questions on tomorrow's quiz
> will come directly from the study guide.

In another classroom, Mr. Labriola begins his lesson by stating the learning
target, providing criteria for success, and alerting students to the performance of
understanding:

> Today we are learning to evaluate the claims used to convince Marcus Brutus
> that Julius Caesar was an enemy of the state who deserved to die. As you read
> today's passage with members of your learning group, identify all the claims
> made by the various conspirators. Then reread the passage to collect evidence

to verify each claim. Remember, to warrant Caesar's death, the claims must be serious and not trivial, and they must be supported by evidence that is reliable and substantiated. Look for evidence that is more than opinion or hearsay. Ask yourself whether the evidence is verifiable—is there a witness or some form of documentation to back up the claim? At the end of the lesson, each group will share three of the claims it investigated, evaluate the quality of the evidence it uncovered, and explain its reasons for deciding whether or not each claim warranted Caesar's death. Each of you has the rubric we will use to weigh the quality of the evidence we find in the play. Note that there are two important elements for evaluating the claims you find: the seriousness of the claim and the reliability of the evidence. Use the rubric as you read, work in your groups, and prepare to share your conclusions. Let's examine the rubric elements now and use them to assess some samples of claims and evidence so we can be sure we understand exactly what the levels of quality on the rubric mean and how they apply.

In Ms. Thompson's lesson, students are flying blind. Even though Ms. Thompson carefully explained expectations and assignment mechanics, her students have few clues about what they are supposed to learn, and learn well, during the lesson. From the students' perspective, it seems like a good idea to concentrate on looking up facts and copying definitions accurately. What the students are actually asked to do does little to help the teacher or her students assess their understanding of essential concepts. The study guide and description of the quiz do little to communicate Ms. Thompson's learning expectations or help students understand what high-quality work looks like for this lesson.

In contrast, everything that happens during Mr. Labriola's lesson converges to make the learning target clear. His introduction, the performance of understanding, the criteria for success, and the description of how students will demonstrate mastery work together to communicate exactly where student learning is headed and what it will take to get there. That's because learning targets and clear criteria for success are driving what happens in this classroom. They focus everything the teacher and students do toward the target.

Keep this tale of two lessons in mind as we examine what we mean by sharing learning targets and explore strategies to do that meaningfully with our students.

WHAT DO WE MEAN BY SHARING THE LEARNING TARGET?

Sharing learning targets with students means more than simply writing the target statement on the board or stating the target at the beginning of the lesson. When we use the term *share,* we mean that teachers use multiple strategies during a formative learning cycle to make sure that students recognize, understand, and aim for what is important to learn during today's lesson. Teachers share the learning target when they embed it throughout today's lesson in ways that keep students "on target" and help them sharpen their aim in pursuit of essential understandings. Sharing the target means that students are engaged in a performance of understanding, use look-fors to assess the quality of their learning, and receive timely suggestions and strategies that feed their learning forward *while* they are learning. Remember, sharing the learning target is the *means*. The desired *end* is students who develop into self-regulated and assessment-capable learners.

In this chapter, we explore how to put the learning target into the minds and hands of our students in ways that make learning visible, develop students' sense of personal agency, and enable them to take responsibility for their own learning throughout the lesson. We also offer suggestions for effective ways to help all students recognize what success looks like for today's lesson.

But first, let's return to Ms. Thompson's lesson on *Julius Caesar* and look at the questions that must be on students' minds:

- What content is important for me to learn?
- Am I supposed to understand the life of William Shakespeare?
- How can I do my best on the study guide?
- I wonder what facts about Julius Caesar are the most important for me to learn.
- Will I be asked to define the archaic words to show that I know what an archaic word means?
- How will I have to do that, and can I use my study guide as a reference?

Sadly, students face lessons like this one each day—lessons designed with the best intentions, guided by broad instructional objectives, and containing a lot of tasks. We stand firmly against defining active engagement on the basis of the number of activities in the lesson. It is what students actively think about—what their minds are on, rather than what their hands are on—that determines active engagement. What we actually require students to do during the lesson should deepen their understanding, produce evidence of their learning, and help them become proficient self-assessors.

Faced with a lesson like Ms. Thompson's, where what the teacher says and what the students are asked to do provide few clues, students expend precious time and energy trying to figure out what their teacher expects of them. Many students, exhausted by the process, wonder why they should even care.

To succeed in today's lesson, students need a specific learning target that describes what they are supposed to learn, a performance of understanding that makes that target visible and gives them the opportunity to aim for it, and clear criteria for success that they can use to take informed steps to improve their learning *while* they are learning.

ENGAGING STUDENTS IN A STRONG PERFORMANCE OF UNDERSTANDING

The single best way to share the learning target and success criteria for today's lesson is through a strong performance of understanding: a learning experience and resulting student performance that embody the learning target and provide compelling evidence of student learning. A strong target-performance match translates the learning target into action. Engaged in a strong performance of understanding, students should be able to conclude, "If I can do this, then I will know I've reached my learning target." Just as important, teachers should be able to conclude, "If my students can do this, then I will have strong evidence that they have reached the learning target."

What we ask students to do during today's lesson should help them make meaning and give them a chance to observe their growing competence. Remember Ms. Thompson's *Julius Caesar* lesson? Her students certainly had a lot to do, but none of the tasks helped them understand what was important to learn or yielded strong evidence of how well they learned it.

A performance of understanding is not the same as an assignment, an activity, a task, or homework. Although a task may be hands-on or interactive, it needs to fulfill important requirements to make the grade as a performance of understanding. "Performance" is only half of the concept. Students can play a match game to connect definitions to vocabulary words, collect leaves, or give a speech without ever developing deep understanding of a concept or producing evidence of how well they know it. The crucial other half of the concept is "understanding." A performance of understanding both develops understanding of the concept and produces evidence that helps students and teachers gauge where that level of understanding resides in relation to the learning target and the success criteria.

A performance of understanding, therefore, is a carefully designed learning experience that happens during the formative learning cycle in today's lesson. Its purpose is to

- Embody the learning target;
- Promote mastery of essential content;
- Develop students' proficiency in specific reasoning skills;
- Provide compelling evidence of student learning; and
- Prepare students for the elevated degree of challenge that will face them in tomorrow's lesson. (Moss et al., 2011c)

Like the fabled glass slipper, a performance of understanding should be such a perfect fit for the learning target and success criteria that the lesson's learning target is crystal clear. Students should be able to recognize what is important to learn, how they will know when they have learned it, and how they will be expected to demonstrate their learning. This perfect fit also means that the level of challenge in today's lesson prepares students for the increased level of challenge they will face in tomorrow's lesson in a different performance of understanding guided by tomorrow's learning target.

INCREASING THE DEGREE OF CHALLENGE

As we observed in Chapter 1, a lesson should never ask students to do more of the same. Lessons should continually challenge students to set, aim for, and reach short-term goals that progressively take them to long-term outcomes.

Let's walk through an example of three lessons designed to help 8th grade language arts students refine their ability to develop an argument. Each lesson is a stepping-stone (short-term goal) toward the long-term goal of being able to successfully engage in a debate. The lessons increasingly challenge students to more competently judge the quality of arguments across a variety of contexts. The learning targets for these lessons reveal a potential learning trajectory that increases students' ability to understand, analyze, and use the three common appeals to reason. Note that as the learning targets become more complex, the performances of understanding become more complex as well, scaffolding the students' understanding and skill.

On Monday, students learn the characteristics of the three persuasive appeals used in argument: logic, emotion, and ethics. The lesson's performance of understanding requires students to work in groups to examine magazine ads and categorize them by the three appeals. Tuesday's lesson will build on what students accomplished Monday and prepare them for Wednesday's challenges.

Tuesday's learning target requires students to create a persuasive argument using one of the three appeals. Working in groups during the performance of understanding, students write a three-minute infomercial using a specific appeal to reason.

Wednesday's learning target increases the challenge again. Students learn to analyze a written argument to identify the different appeals used by the author. During Wednesday's performance of understanding, students read an essay arguing for year-round schools and identify the extent to which the essay uses each type of appeal.

As you consider the potential learning trajectory of the three lessons, think of the metaphor of aiming for a target. Each lesson's performance of understanding places the bow and arrow into students' hands and gives them ample opportunities to sharpen their aim. These opportunities can happen over a series of lessons, but each opportunity is unique in that it builds on the degree of challenge.

DEFINING AND DESIGNING STRONG CRITERIA FOR SUCCESS

Even with a strong performance of understanding, students cannot become sharpshooters until they are able to discern the levels in quality that differentiate hitting the bull's-eye dead center from hitting one of the target's outer rings. To hit the bull's-eye, students need criteria for success—a set of student look-fors—to use during the formative learning cycle in today's lesson and to apply during the performance of understanding.

To be useful, the criteria must be specific to the learning target, understandable, and visible. Success criteria answer an important question about the lesson from the student's point of view: "How will I know when I hit my learning target?" Many educators mistakenly assume that they are sharing success criteria when they tell their students how many questions they should get right on an assignment or encourage them to shoot for a certain score or simply to "do their best." These vague criteria cannot foster the kind of meaningful goal setting or critical self-assessment that our theory of action requires.

Success criteria are not ways to certify student understanding in terms of grading language: scores (55/60), grades (*A*+), percentages (95%), or any other numbers or labels. Rather, they describe what it means to do quality work in today's lesson in student-friendly terms that are "lesson-sized," observable, and measurable. Students can use the criteria to plan, monitor, and assess their own learning progress.

A helpful way to think about success criteria is to envision an actual target, like the one in Figure 3.1. The bull's-eye, dead center, depicts mastery—what students will aim for and what success looks like when students hit their learning target. The target's outer rings represent the typical levels of understanding we expect to see as students move closer toward mastery—proficient, basic, or minimal.

3.1 Success Criteria Define the Rings That Make Up the Learning Target

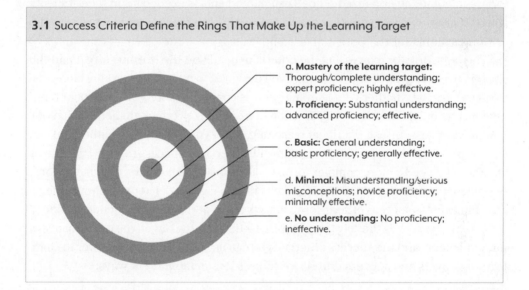

a. **Mastery of the learning target:** Thorough/complete understanding; expert proficiency; highly effective.

b. **Proficiency:** Substantial understanding; advanced proficiency; effective.

c. **Basic:** General understanding; basic proficiency; generally effective.

d. **Minimal:** Misunderstanding/serious misconceptions; novice proficiency; minimally effective.

e. **No understanding:** No proficiency; ineffective.

Once you craft the specific learning target statement for today's lesson, consider what growing understanding and competence will look like for students as they progress from little or minimal understanding toward a more sophisticated grasp of the content. Think about how typical learning progress plays out for your students (at their age and developmental levels) in this chunk of content and during this performance of understanding. How will you describe mastery to them so that they will be able to tell when they hit the bull's-eye? How will they know where they are in relation to mastery—the distance between their performance and the bull's-eye—so that they can assess their progress?

Useful success criteria can take many forms, but they must do two things really well: they must fit the performance of understanding, and they must make effective teaching and meaningful learning visible. Strong criteria precisely describe what good work looks like for the specific performance of understanding in the lesson. It makes perfect sense. We designed the performance of understanding by considering the learning intention—the specific content plus the potential learning trajectory for the lesson—and the learning target.

Make sure to frame and organize the success criteria from the students' point of view. For younger students, "I can" statements are particularly useful, but they also help older students. Sometimes one-sentence "I can" statements are sufficient as criteria; sometimes an organized set of "I can" statements is needed to provide students with the most useful description of success (e.g., "I can create a product with all the attributes in this rubric").

The best form for expressing the criteria depends on the learning target and the specific performance of understanding you designed to make that learning target visible. First, decide whether your learning target is comprehension of a concept or term, demonstration of a discrete skill, creation of a complex product, demonstration of a complex process, or use of critical reasoning. Then you will know whether you can use simple "I can" statements to communicate criteria for success to your students or whether you need a more complex format—like rubrics, exemplars, demonstrations, or guided questions—to communicate the criteria. Figure 3.2 illustrates how to organize and express success criteria for various types of performances of understanding.

Now that you have the "big three" in place—the learning target, the performance of understanding, and the success criteria—you can use their combined power to share learning targets and success criteria for today's lesson in different ways.

SHARING THE LEARNING TARGET AND SUCCESS CRITERIA VERBALLY

Verbally sharing the learning target and success criteria means more than simply telling students what to do in the lesson. To be effective, the language we use must be descriptive, specific, developmentally appropriate, and student-friendly. And it must

3.2 Tailoring the Criteria for Success to the Performance of Understanding

If the performance of understanding involves . . .	Examples	Then useful criteria for success might be . . .
Grasping a new concept or term.	• Science: weather front, DNA, ecosystem. • Social studies: state capitals, government, imperialism, urbanization. • Language arts: parts of speech, nonfiction, root word. • Mathematics: integer, volume, estimation, prediction. • Music: tempo, timbre, controlled breathing.	**Organized as "I can" statements:** • I can explain [concept or term] in my own words. • I can give examples of what [concept or term] is and examples of what [concept or term] is not. • I can use [concept or term] to analyze a situation [or text, or data] or to solve a problem.
Demonstrating a discrete skill—a brief, well-defined action that has a clear beginning and end.	• Graphing a quadratic equation. • Shooting a free throw. • Forming a contraction. • Changing a sentence from passive to active voice. • Measuring the circumference of a circle. • Tying my shoe.	**Organized as an "I can" statements checklist of important elements, steps, or rules of the skill:** I can change a passive sentence into an active sentence by • Turning the object of the passive sentence into the "star," or the subject, of the active sentence. • Removing the "to be" form, "en," or "ed" from the passive verb to make it an active verb. • Turning the subject of the passive sentence into the direct object of the active sentence.

continued

3.2 Tailoring the Criteria for Success to the Performance of Understanding (*continued*)

If the performance of understanding involves . . .	Examples	Then useful criteria for success might be . . .
Creating a complex product or demonstrating a complex process.	• Writing a descriptive paragraph. • Participating in a debate. • Creating a PowerPoint presentation. • Planting a terrarium. • Outlining a book chapter. • Demonstrating how to call 911. • Giving an informative speech. • Writing a piece of fan fiction. • Writing a letter to my state congressperson.	**Organized as a rubric:** I can [write a piece of fan fiction, plant a terrarium] according to the descriptions in the rubric. **Embodied in examples of good work:** I can [write a descriptive paragraph, create a PowerPoint presentation] that is as good as this one because . . . **Demonstrated through expert modeling of the process:** I can [give an informative speech, call 911] just as well as [modeler of process] did because . . .
Using critical, creative, or self-regulatory reasoning processes and thinking skills to maximize the quality of a performance or product.	• Classifying the eight planets in an original way. • Describing the similarities and differences between prose and poetry. • Writing an essay that argues for wind power over fossil fuels. • Identifying the general pattern of a song and then finding songs that share that pattern. • Setting three goals for improving my diet. • Inventing a better way to line up for the bus.	**Organized as guiding questions for the reasoning process:** I can use my best thinking to classify the planets by asking myself these questions: • Can I identify the things I am going to classify? • Can I name something important that these things have in common and use it to create a category? • Can I state the rule that describes what the things in this group have in common? • Is there anything that does not belong to this group? Can I make another category for some of the things that do not belong?

be stated from the point of view of a student who has not yet mastered the learning target. Two strategies promote effective verbal sharing: the Four-Step Framework and the I-Can Framework. A third strategy—listening to students as they paraphrase the target—deepens student understanding when used in conjunction with either oral sharing framework.

The Four-Step Framework

This framework employs a set of "starter prompts" that unpack the learning target, performance of understanding, and success criteria from the student's point of view (see Figure 3.3, p. 52). The successive steps of the framework outline what students will learn during today's lesson, explain what they will do to learn it, describe what they will look for to know they are doing good work, and make the target relevant by connecting it to the potential learning trajectory, future academic learning, or real-world applications.

The four starter prompts of the framework are

- We are learning to . . .
- We will show that we can do this by . . .
- To know how well we are learning this, we will look for . . .
- It is important for us to learn this (or be able to do this) because . . .

We'll use a 3rd grade language arts lesson to illustrate how the four prompts work together to share the learning target with students. The teacher's learning target for the lesson is "Students will learn how to sequence the four main events of a story."

Step 1. Explain the learning target in student-friendly, developmentally appropriate terms: *We are learning to* put the four most important events of a story we read into the exact order they happened in the story to answer the question "What happened first, second, third, and last?"

Step 2. Describe the performance of understanding: *We will show that we can do this by* placing pictures of the four important events from the story in the exact order we remember them happening.

Step 3. Describe the student look-fors: *To know how well we are learning this, we will look for* the match between the order of our pictures and the sequence of events in the story as we reread it.

3.3 The Four-Step Framework

The learning target for today's lesson: _____

Steps	What the Teacher Says
Step 1: Explain the learning target in student-friendly, developmentally appropriate terms.	We are learning to . . .
Step 2: Describe the performance of understanding.	We will show that we can do this by . . .
Step 3: Describe the student look-fors.	To know how well we are learning this, we will look for . . .
Step 4: Make it relevant.	It is important for us to learn this because . . .

Step 4. Make it relevant: *It is important for us to be able to* put what happens in a story in the right order because it helps us understand and remember stories and books we read. It will help us in our next lesson when we learn how to write our own stories. Knowing and remembering the order of important events also helps us learn science, history, math, and other subjects in school. It is a skill we will use for the rest of our lives, no matter what we do when we grow up. Doctors, detectives, teachers, mechanics, musicians, chefs, and many others must know and follow the exact order of things.

The I-Can Framework

This strategy pairs a description of the learning target with an "I can" statement that describes the performance of understanding for today's lesson and translates the criteria for success into look-fors that students can understand and use. You can complete the starter prompts of the framework to fit your students' grade level and the lesson content. The following example uses the framework in the context of a high school lesson on writing a thesis statement for a persuasive speech.

Step 1. Use the first starter prompt to describe the learning target: *We are learning to* create an effective thesis statement for a persuasive speech that sums up what we want our audience to do, feel, think, or agree with.

Step 2. Use the second starter prompt to alert students to the performance of understanding as an "I can" statement. The statement should tell students what they will do to deepen and demonstrate their understanding and provide a short list of student look-fors that explain how well they are expected to do it. You will know you are able to do this when you are able to say "I can" write a thesis statement that

- Is simple, clear, and direct.
- Says what's important.
- Is easy to remember and understand.
- Announces what the audience should do, feel, think, or agree with.
- Explains a benefit for the audience.

Figure 3.4 (p. 54) provides examples of the I-Can Framework for a middle school and an elementary school lesson.

Listening to Students as They Paraphrase the Learning Target

You can boost the effect of either verbal sharing framework by asking your students to paraphrase the learning target and success criteria. After you use one of the frameworks, ask students to spend three to five minutes putting the target and the student look-fors into their own words. Then ask them to use the look-fors to talk about where they are on their way to the learning target. Students can do this with a peer, in a learning group, or as a class to make sure everyone understands.

Rubrics are excellent tools for sharing learning targets that are parts of complex concepts, processes, or skills. Some complex understandings can be accomplished in one lesson, but most require teachers to scaffold student understanding across a series of interrelated lessons. A well-designed rubric is a highly effective way to share the learning target used for today's lesson or the connected learning targets used across a series of lessons to build mastery. Rubrics help students aim for understanding and set goals for individual performances of understanding as they move from naïve to more sophisticated levels of content knowledge, and from basic skills to proficiency.

3.4 The I-Can Framework

Level and Topic	Describe the Learning Target	Use "I Can" Statements to Share the Performance of Understanding and Student Look-fors
Middle School: Assassination of President John F. Kennedy	*We are learning to* perform a historical investigation that examines a past event to determine what happened, why it happened, and why people still disagree about it to this day.	*You will know you can do this when you are able to say:* *I can* use the steps of the historical investigation process to answer these questions about the assassination of President John F. Kennedy: • What do people already know? • What is it that people cannot know for sure? • What specific disagreements do people have about what happened? • What evidence exists to support the two sides of the disagreement?
Elementary School: Proper nouns	*We are learning to* find proper nouns in a story.	*You will know you can do this when you are able to say:* *I can* read a story and circle all the proper nouns I find.

USING RUBRICS TO SHARE CONNECTED LEARNING TARGETS AND SUC-CESS CRITERIA. Connected learning targets help students reach complex learning outcomes like writing a persuasive essay, charting the effects of earthquakes on buildings, researching the history and culture behind a favorite family recipe, tracking the life of a legislative bill, describing a typical day in the life of a specific community helper, or calculating the profit from selling a pitcher of lemonade. These complex learning outcomes usually require more than one lesson and develop over a series of lessons as part of a potential learning trajectory.

A quality rubric, especially an analytic rubric, stipulates the essential elements of a complex performance and describes the levels of quality (success criteria) for each element. A series of lessons, then, can take students through the different elements of the complex performance to help them put it all together in the end. Quality rubrics allow the teacher *and* the students to assess exactly where students are and to select strategies that students can use to improve their work. A rubric for a complex performance also helps students set and aim for short-term goals for today's lesson (*I will write a strong thesis statement*) and build toward long-term goals (*I will write a comprehensive and well-supported research paper*).

There are countless ways to use rubrics before, during, and after a lesson to share the learning targets and success criteria for a particular performance of understanding. Figure 3.5 (p. 56) provides several such strategies.

USING RUBRICS TO EXAMINE EXEMPLARS OF SUCCESSFUL AND UNSUCCESSFUL WORK. An effective way to share the learning target and help students discern different levels of quality of work—a process that moves them closer to being assessment-capable—is to ask students to apply a rubric to work samples that match the performance of understanding for today's lesson. You can either collect papers or products from past students to share anonymously or create examples to represent various levels of quality—examples where the work is successful or flawed in one or several areas.

If the performance of understanding involves something other than a tangible product—giving a speech, playing an instrument, or dribbling a basketball, for example—you can use video to capture performances that demonstrate varying levels of quality. It's best to create the performances from scratch by either modeling the performances yourself or using unknown students as the performers.

Ask students to examine the work samples or observe the performances using the criteria in the rubric. Students should underline or highlight the exact language in the rubric that describes the quality of the work. Then, in groups or as a whole class, students should share their assessments using the language from the rubrics to support their judgments. As an alternative or complementary activity, have students sort the products or performances into different levels of quality and then explain their rankings using the language from the rubric you provided or from one they created themselves.

Students who examine examples of work against criteria in a rubric will be better able to assess their own performances. They will develop a more nuanced view of what quality work looks like for today's lesson and use that knowledge during the performance of understanding.

3.5 Using Rubrics to Share the Learning Target and Criteria for Success

Strategy	How to Use the Strategy
Ready, Steady, Pair-Share	1. Give the rubric to students before a performance of understanding. 2. Students sit with a partner and take turns explaining the elements in the rubric. 3. Students begin the performance of understanding. 4. Halfway through the performance, students return to their pairs and explain how what they are doing meets the criteria for success in the rubric. 5. Students repeat step 3 at the end of the performance of understanding.
Strategic Goal Setting	1. Give the rubric to students before a performance of understanding. 2. Students plan and list strategies for a successful performance, one strategy for each element in the rubric.
"Traffic Light" Student Self-Assessment (based on Atkin, Black, & Coffey, 2001; Black, Harrison, Lee, Marshall, & Wiliam, 2002)	1. Give students a copy of the rubric. 2. Students work in pairs to discuss their understanding of the rubric. 3. Students engage in their performance of understanding. 4. At the midpoint of the performance, students stop and "traffic light" where they are using the rubric and red, green, and yellow dots to mark where they think their work is now: — Green = solid understanding—I'm ready to go. — Yellow = partial understanding—I need to slow down and think about this carefully. — Red = I need help and can't do this on my own. 5. Students with green dots help the students with yellow dots in a specific area. 6. The teacher groups students with common red dots to reteach the skill or content.

Strategy	How to Use the Strategy
I Can . . . Now I Can Self-Assessment	1. Give the rubric to students. 2. Partway through the lesson or task, ask students to mark the level of the rubric that shows their present level of performance—their "I can." 3. Ask students to list a strategy for an area where they should improve or revise their work. 4. At the end of the lesson or task, ask students to mark the rubric with a different color to show how their strategies helped improve their work— "Now I can."
Teacher-Student Assess and Compare	1. Give the rubric to students. 2. Students use a yellow highlighter to mark the levels in the rubric that best describe how they assess their performance. 3. The teacher assesses each student's performance using the student's rubric and a blue highlighter. 4. The places where "yellow and blue make green" show agreement on the student's application of the criteria for success. 5. Areas that remain blue are places where the teacher can help the student better understand the criteria.
Student-Made Rubric	1. Give students a blank table or template for a rubric. 2. As a whole class or in small groups, ask students what constitutes good work for the lesson (good writing, good eye contact, good participation, etc.). Students will use this list as the elements of their rubric. 3. Ask students to create descriptions of strong and weak work for each element to create a simple rubric.

ASKING TARGETED WARM-UP QUESTIONS. We commonly use warm-up exercises before physical activity to prepare our bodies for optimal performance. Think of targeted warm-up questions (Sato & Atkin, 2006/2007) in the same way. These questions share the learning target for today's lesson to trigger student thinking about what they are going to learn, how they will be asked to demonstrate their learning, and what good work will look like.

Targeted warm-up questions are not something a teacher can ad-lib; they take time to prepare. Begin by writing two or three questions to help your students review what they learned in yesterday's lesson (*What strategies can we use to write a strong topic sentence?*). This helps students connect the current lesson with the potential learning trajectory. Then prepare a set of questions that focus students on what they will learn in today's lesson, the performance of understanding, and the success criteria (*How will our topic sentence help us plan the other sentences in our descriptive paragraph?*).

The idea is to lead a discussion on how today's lesson will help students aim for and hit the learning target. The discussion should preview how the lesson will progress and help students picture how they will work to construct the way forward.

SHARING LEARNING TARGETS THROUGH HOMEWORK

Homework is not a performance of understanding, and we shouldn't treat it as such. It is never a good idea to rely on homework as the sole vehicle for sharing the learning target or as the primary evidence of what students know and can do in relation to the learning target. The power of a performance of understanding is that it happens in today's lesson during a formative learning cycle to foster student understanding, self-assessment, and goal setting. Most important, the performance is guided by the teacher's up-to-the-minute feedback and scaffolding.

Likewise, homework should never ask students to learn something new on their own or do something that confuses them. If students cannot successfully complete a math problem under your guidance, assigning 30 similar problems for homework won't help. Rather than hoping that practice at home will make perfect, realize that practice makes permanent! Struggling with those problems for homework means that misconceptions and points of confusion will become firmly implanted. Students should learn new concepts and processes during today's lesson in partnership with their teacher.

An effective homework task, however, *can* be used to share the learning target when what we ask students to do at home extends what we ask them to do during the lesson to reach the learning target. Students should "have no trouble connecting homework to classroom learning" (Vatterott, 2009, p. 101). That means they should already understand the learning target and their potential learning trajectory. You can design a great homework assignment by using the same learning target you used to design today's lesson and the evidence of student progress you gathered during the performance of understanding. Just remember: homework shares the learning target only when it asks students to practice and review what they *already know and understand.*

HOW DO LEARNING TARGETS INCREASE STUDENT MOTIVATION TO LEARN?

When students understand the lesson's learning target, the performance that will demonstrate their understanding, and the criteria by which their work will be assessed, they improve their ability to self-regulate. Self-regulating students continually monitor their progress toward a goal, check outcomes, and redirect unsuccessful efforts (Berk, 2003). Students who self-regulate no longer view learning as a covert event that happens *to* them as a result of instruction controlled by their teacher. Rather, they view learning as an activity they do for themselves and that is under *their* control (Zimmerman, 2001). Self-regulation fuses *skill* and *will* and develops as students learn to plan, control, and evaluate their own success within a specific context. A self-regulated learner knows how to learn, knows his or her potential and limitations for the task at hand, and can adjust his or her behavior to optimize success (Montalvo & Gonzalez Torres, 2004).

Self-regulation—the motivational energy students need to aim toward mastery in a lesson—requires an understanding of the learning target *and* the criteria for success. If students have no understanding of the learning target, like the students muddling through Ms. Thompson's lesson on *Julius Caesar,* they will flounder and perhaps quit, or at least quit caring. If students understand *only* the learning target, they can envision where they are headed but will have little confidence in their ability to get there.

In contrast, understanding the learning target *and* the success criteria as they engage in a strong performance of understanding puts students in the driver's seat. They know where they are going, can assess where they are, are able to monitor their work, and can select strategies to help them do their best. Because both halves of the learning team know exactly how student work will be assessed during the lesson, there are no surprises. Whether students are solving a story problem using fractions with like denominators, creating a self-sustaining ecosystem, or translating a piece of French poetry into English, they can monitor how they are doing and make adjustments to close in on the learning target. They know not only what they have to do but also how they have to do it to succeed. That knowledge enhances their motivation to learn.

LOOKING FORWARD

Learning targets inform the most important data-driven decision maker in the classroom—the student—by providing information about what is important to learn, how the student will be required to demonstrate that learning, and what will count as evidence of mastery.

In Chapter 4, we consider how teachers can use learning targets during a formative learning cycle to make teaching and learning visible, maximize opportunities to feed students forward, and increase student achievement.

4

USING LEARNING TARGETS TO FEED LEARNING FORWARD

When you teach someone how to drive, your teaching begins before you get into the car. You consider what the student driver needs to master during today's lesson according to your long-term goals and the evidence you gathered from the last lesson. You choose a destination and a driving route that represent the appropriate level of challenge.

With your student behind the wheel, you explain and model one or two particular skills that he should aim for as he drives. You describe the exact route, noting lane changes and sharp turns that lie ahead and suggesting specific strategies for negotiating these lane changes and turns. These strategies will help your student stay safely on the road and boost his confidence for meeting upcoming challenges.

As the student drives the targeted route, you both pay close attention to his decisions and performance. You provide crucial criteria that help him keep track of how well he is doing as he is driving. If he drifts off course, you supply a "just-in-time" strategy to keep him firmly on the road. If he is unable to safely continue, you have him pull over and stop. You discuss what he did and how well he did it, and you use that information to reteach the concepts and skills he needs to learn to move forward. Before he continues driving, you provide a refined set of skills and strategies that he can use to improve his driving. Throughout the lesson, you partner with him to aim for today's learning target and work toward the long-term goal of becoming a capable, self-regulated, and independent driver.

This driving lesson's combination of learning targets, long-term goals, and feedback that feeds forward is exactly what all students need to achieve more. In this chapter, we examine how feeding students' learning forward—that is, using learning targets to show students where "forward" is and using feedback to help them get there—leads to improved student achievement.

To begin, we examine the influential role of the classroom learning team. Feeding students forward is not a one-way street; it requires teachers to forge a learning partnership with their students. Next, we explore the characteristics of feedback that feeds forward: what it is, when it happens, and why it matters. We then describe the relationship between feedback that feeds forward and specific, appropriate, and challenging learning goals. Finally, we illustrate how to maximize opportunities to feed learning forward during a formative learning cycle.

THE POWER OF THE CLASSROOM LEARNING TEAM

What students actually do during today's lesson, when guided by an expert teacher, has an enormous influence on their achievement. In fact, research has found that "most students can reach the same level of achievement as the top 20% of students" (Bellon, Bellon, & Blank, 1992, pp. 277–278).

Of the factors that have the greatest influence on student achievement, 20 percent are spread across hundreds of factors, including testing methods; the physical arrangement of classrooms; peer influences; and students' learning styles, socioeconomic status, and home lives. Students' cognitive ability and past experiences account for another 50 percent of the factors. Finally, teacher expertise—what teachers do and how they do it—accounts for the remaining 30 percent of the factors that influence student achievement (Hattie, 2002, 2009). No other single educational factor comes close. Clearly, what teachers do matters.

Expert teachers have deep content knowledge and a deep understanding of how best to teach that content. They consistently make better decisions than less-expert teachers about the learning targets they design and share, the degree of challenge they build into today's lesson, the long- and short-term goals they set for their students, and the opportunities they employ to feed learning forward. Because they more skillfully monitor and assess student performances, they are able to provide highly effective feedback.

As they plan today's lesson, expert teachers consider what typical (and not-so-typical) student progress looks like for the lesson's content and design a range of specific learning strategies that they can use to help students move toward mastery. They create an appropriate degree of challenge in their lessons and prepare for student successes and struggles. Their strategic foresight doesn't eliminate unforeseen problems; rather, it prepares them to capitalize on feed-forward opportunities throughout today's lesson. Expert teachers spend more of the lesson engaging their students in challenging tasks that encourage students to commit to the target. In contrast, less-expert teachers spend 80 percent of a lesson talking while their students passively listen (Hattie, 2002).

Of course, effective feedback doesn't always move from the teacher to the student. During a formative learning cycle, *both* halves of the learning team gather evidence of student progress and use that evidence to improve what they do. When students are trying on the learning target and applying the success criteria with their teacher, they produce evidence—feedback to the teacher—of what they understand and can do.

CHARACTERISTICS OF FEEDBACK THAT FEEDS FORWARD

Effective feedback more strongly and consistently raises student achievement than any other teaching behavior (Hattie, 2009). It provides students with "just-in-time, just-for-me information delivered when and where it can do the most good" (Brookhart, 2008, p. 1), and it answers the three central questions of the formative assessment process from the student's point of view:

1. What knowledge or skills form my learning target for this lesson?

2. How close am I to mastering them?

3. What do I need to do next to close the gap?

To put feedback that feeds forward into context, let's look at a 5th grade math lesson. Here are the lesson's learning target and success criteria:

We are learning to use models to show how we can use a ratio to compare two or more quantities. We will know that we are able to do this when we are able to say, I can use the "number : number" format to write ratios for the model that compare part to part, whole to part, and part to whole.

Everything the teacher does during this lesson helps students recognize what they currently understand about how to write ratios for the model, set goals for what they need to learn or do next to be able to use ratios to compare quantities, use specific look-fors to monitor their ability to write ratios for the model, and use the evidence they gather to become better at using ratios to compare quantities.

Feedback That Feeds Forward Has Nutritional Value

Good food has nutritional value; it feeds our bodies. Think of effective feedback in the same way: it must have nutritional value to "feed" students forward. Stickers, grades (*B+*), marks (25/30), scores (87%), or general, value-laden comments ("Good for you" or "Try harder") have no nutritional value—no information that students can use to set goals for improvement and choose effective strategies to meet those goals.

Effective feedback is nonjudgmental, positive, and descriptive. It arrives *while* students are learning so that they can use it to improve their work (Brookhart, 2008; Moss & Brookhart, 2009). Feedback that feeds forward shares five characteristics:

1. It focuses on success criteria from the learning target for today's lesson.

2. It describes exactly where the student is in relationship to the criteria.

3. It provides a next-step strategy that the student should use to improve or learn more.

4. It arrives when the student has the opportunity to use it.

5. It is delivered in just the right amount—not so much that it overwhelms, but not so little that it stops short of a useful explanation or suggestion.

Figure 4.1 sets these characteristics within the context of a nutritional value chart.

4.1 Feed-Forward Nutritional Chart

Feed-Forward Nutritional Value
Serving Size: Feedback on today's performance
of understanding

Amount: "Just right"

	% of Nutritional Value
What % of your feedback information...	
Compares what the student did with the learning target for today's lesson?	_____
Describes what the student did well?	_____
Suggests a specific next-step strategy?	_____
Arrived during or close to the performance of understanding so that the student had a chance to use it to improve his or her work?	_____
Uses developmentally appropriate, student-friendly success criteria language that the student understands?	_____

Source: From *Advancing Formative Assessment in Every Classroom: A Guide for Instructional Leaders* (p. 55), by C. M. Moss and S. M. Brookhart, 2009, Alexandria, VA: ASCD. Adapted with permission.

The Mirror and the Magnet in the Meaningful Moment: Another Way to Think About Feedback That Feeds Forward

Feeding students forward helps them recognize the quality of their work and what they should do next to succeed while they still have time to use feedback to improve. The metaphor of "the mirror and the magnet in the meaningful moment" is a great way to envision this process.

- **The mirror.** Acting as a mirror, effective feedback provides an accurate picture of where the student is in comparison to where she needs to go. The student should be able to say, "Here is my distance from the learning target. I can tell where I am because these are the things I can do well, and these are the things I have yet to master." Your purpose is to describe what the student does well and identify a specific area where she can improve: "Renata, you followed each of the four steps for reading a contour map. Two of your altitudes are misinterpreted. Your next step should be to focus on your map-reading accuracy."

- **The magnet.** Once your feedback mirrors the student's strengths and reveals exactly where she can improve, you are ready to use your feedback as a magnet to pull her forward. Provide the student with a logical, next-step strategy that considers what she can do well and what she should do to improve: "Renata, here is a strategy you can use to improve your accuracy when you interpret a contour map. The key is to pay special attention to the altitudes of each contour layer, because every point on a contour line represents the exact same elevation. Moving from one contour line to another always means a change in elevation. To figure out whether it is positive (uphill) or negative (downhill), look at the index contours on either side."

- **The meaningful moment.** Describing where a student is and providing specific suggestions for what she should do next have little impact if the meaningful moment has already passed. Your feedback should arrive while your student still has the opportunity to use it to improve her performance. The combination of feed-forward information and the opportunity to use that information is what gives your feedback nutritional value. The fresher the food, the higher the nutrients, and the more timely the feedback, the more chance it has to influence student achievement.

Feedback That Feeds Forward Fosters Student Goal Setting

Feedback that feeds forward helps students both *get* smarter and *learn* smarter by engaging them in targeted goal setting, a cognitive process that enhances achievement and motivation to learn—especially when the goal setters have some control over the outcome (Locke & Latham, 2006). The most successful students take charge of their own learning (Ormrod, 2011a), viewing it as an activity they do for themselves in a proactive, self-regulated manner (Zimmerman, 2001). An upward cycle of learning happens "when students confidently set learning goals that are moderately challenging yet realistic, and then exert the effort, energy, and resources needed to accomplish those goals" (Rolheiser, Bower, & Stevahn, 2000, p. 35). The kind of goals that students set and work toward determines how they approach their learning.

All students want to achieve and do their best. But the reason *why* they want to achieve determines how they define achievement. In other words, *what* they mean by doing their best and *how* they go about getting there depend on the goal they have in mind for themselves—the *why*. The two types of goals we discuss here are performance goals and mastery goals.

PERFORMANCE GOALS. Some students frame their "why" as a performance goal. They want to "look smart to themselves and others and avoid looking dumb" (Dweck, 2000, p. 15): *I'm going to get an A on my essay to show my class what a great writer I am.* These students are more extrinsically motivated and rely on rewards or praise from others. Because their main desire is to make a good impression, they tend to avoid mistakes at all cost, sometimes cutting corners to do so. For example, they will memorize vocabulary definitions rather than work to understand important concepts. When given the chance, they choose a safe level of challenge: in basketball terms, either taking the shot directly under the net where they are sure to make it, or attempting an impossible shot from the other end of the court that would impress everyone should they sink it but cause no shame if they miss. These students rely on rote learning strategies like repetition, copying, and memorization. They measure their progress according to others' and seek feedback that flatters them.

Performance goals are a part of life, and we are certainly not suggesting that wanting to get a good grade is uncommon or trivial. What we are suggesting, however, is that when students aim solely for performance goals (*I have to know this because it is going to be on the test*), their learning tends to be superficial and short-lived rather than meaningful and enduring.

MASTERY GOALS. Mastery goals help students frame their learning from a different angle: the "why" that motivates them is the desire to increase their competence, to "get smarter" (Dweck, 2000, p. 15) by mastering new knowledge or skills.

Focused by mastery goals, students understand that it takes effort over time to understand complex concepts and become skilled at a process or procedure. Mastery goals help students realize that they will not be experts on day one. Students who aim for mastery goals tend to challenge themselves to apply what they learn, to regard mistakes as inevitable, and to capitalize on errors as important sources of feedback. They tend to be autonomous, intrinsically motivated, and more productive than are students who aim exclusively for performance goals (Locke & Latham, 2002). They prefer appropriately challenging tasks—neither too easy nor too out of reach—and expect to receive feedback on how well they are doing and how to improve. They find learning activities meaningful and strive to get the maximum benefits from them (Brophy, 2004). They judge their progress against targeted criteria, not against the progress of others.

TEACHING EFFECTIVE GOAL SETTING DURING TODAY'S LESSON. Effective goal setting is not a natural part of what students learn to do in school. Sadly, by the time most students reach middle school, they are poorly equipped to set effective goals, unable to anticipate the consequences of their decisions, armed with general and ineffective learning strategies, and unprepared to deal with setbacks in a self-directed way (Zimmerman & Cleary, 2006).

By design, a learning target focuses on what is important for students to *learn* today and on the criteria they will use to assess the quality of their learning—not on the score or grade they should aim for. The distinction between a learning target and a grade is crucial. We are not suggesting that grades are unimportant; what we *are* suggesting is that when teachers encourage students to work toward a certain grade rather than to strive to master the important content that will yield that grade, they are selling their students short.

You can teach your students to value and set mastery goals by consistently feeding them forward toward their learning target. Use descriptive language that describes what they are about to learn, and give them specific look-fors to help them assess their progress toward the learning target as they engage in the performance of understanding. The level of your students' achievement will correlate with the degree to which you partner with them in pursuit of specific learning targets (rather than general "do-your-best" goals).

Finally, keep in mind that although it is important to help students commit to your goals and learn how to set goals of their own, the most important factor is the level of challenge you set for today's lesson (Locke & Latham, 1990). Teaching students to set goals that will not move them forward is an exercise in futility. Make sure that your words, actions, assignments, and assessments demonstrate that you value conceptual understanding and increased skill.

Feedback That Feeds Forward Increases Self-Efficacy

Feeding students forward teaches them to recognize challenges, take steps to meet them, and set challenging goals of their own. It also increases students' sense of self-efficacy —a motivational factor that plays a major role in how they approach goals, tasks, and challenges.

Students with a high sense of self-efficacy believe that they can perform well and are more likely to view difficult tasks as challenges to be mastered rather than avoided and to persevere in tackling those tasks (Bandura, 1997; Pajares, 2006). These students are more likely to use effective self-regulatory skills and learning strategies like self-monitoring, time management, self-assessment, and strategic help-seeking (Zimmerman, Bonner, & Kovach, 1996). The best way to help students develop these productive habits of mind is to feed their learning forward during a formative learning cycle.

Self-efficacy is task- and situation-specific. For example, a student may have high self-efficacy for balancing chemical equations and low self-efficacy for translating a passage into French. Students increase their perceptions of self-efficacy by tackling appropriate levels of challenge in specific areas and by attributing their success to the decisions they make and the strategies they use. Your feedback should help students prepare for, work through, and master the content and skills that make up the learning target for today's lesson.

FEEDING LEARNING FORWARD DURING A FORMATIVE LEARNING CYCLE

A formative learning cycle is a high-leverage process that brings the learning target theory of action to life. It fuses feed-forward information and goal-directed learning with the power of the classroom learning team. As illustrated in Figure 1.6 (p. 22), a formative learning cycle has five general phases:

1. Model and explain.

2. Scaffold learning, goal setting, and self-assessment through guided practice.

3. Engage students in a performance of understanding.

4. Provide formative feedback.

5. Give students the opportunity to use the feedback to improve their performance.

The learning target figures prominently during each phase: it defines where "forward" is for today's lesson so that both halves of the learning team can aim for it. The learning target is the reference point for the feed-forward information you provide to your students throughout the lesson as you partner with them to master essential content, recognize the learning challenges and the strategies they will use to meet them, monitor their progress, assess their understanding against specific criteria, and sustain their engagement over the long run.

In the following sections, we examine each phase of the formative learning cycle and show how to maximize opportunities to feed students forward throughout today's lesson. For each phase we provide an overview of the intended outcome; questions to guide your planning, teaching, and self-improvement efforts; and a classroom example.

Phase One: Model and Explain

Your mission: Model and explain the learning intention for today's lesson by sharing the learning target, success criteria, and performance of understanding.

To achieve this mission,

- Use goal-directed language that encourages students to set mastery goals for what they will learn and how well they will learn it. *How can I explain and model the learning intention for today's lesson to eliminate distractions and focus my students squarely on where we are headed? How can I explain the success criteria in a way that enables students to gauge what they do and do not understand? How can I help students set specific goals for what they need to learn, what they will do to learn it, and how well they should do it? How can I model and explain the level of challenge in today's lesson to encourage students' commitment to their goals?*
- Dig into your expertise about teaching this content to identify the errors students typically make or concepts that confuse them. *What concepts and skills are crucial for students to master to meet the challenge in today's lesson*

and prepare for tomorrow's lesson? What are the typical errors students make? Which concepts do they typically confuse or misunderstand?

- Explain the content or process in a way that draws students' attention to trouble spots and helps them avoid misconception traps. *What misconceptions or points of confusion usually derail student success with this specific content? How can I explain this content to nip misconceptions in the bud?*
- Name and model content-specific strategies they can use. *What specific strategies can I teach students to avoid confusion? How can I point out ways in which the strategies will help them reach today's learning target?*
- Gather evidence of student learning. *What evidence can I gather from my students to determine what I am explaining and modeling well and not so well? What should I re-explain, and to whom should I re-explain it? Have I made the learning target and success criteria visible so that my students and I can use them during guided practice? If I ask several students what is important to learn in today's lesson and how they will know whether they have learned it, can they respond with descriptive language and success criteria?*

Example: Mr. Boyko's 10th grade history class will learn how to investigate historical artifacts to understand the plight of the Cambodian Boat People. Mr. Boyko knows that students typically confuse the two concepts of *immigration* and *emigration,* and those terms appear throughout the artifacts. As he explains the learning intention for the lesson, Mr. Boyko uses goal-directed, descriptive language to draw students' attention to the challenge and provides a specific strategy students can use to avoid the mix-up: "There are two concepts that are important for us to master so that we can better understand the consequences faced by the Cambodian Boat People who fled the Khmer Rouge and sought asylum in Australia. These concepts—*immigration* and *emigration*—sound similar, look a bit alike, and have definitions that can be confusing because they describe a similar action from two different perspectives. *Emigration* is the act of leaving your home country to go to another country. Notice it starts with the letter *E*—the same letter that starts the word *exit.* When you see the *E* at the beginning of *emigration,* think of exiting your homeland to go to another country. *Immigration* is the act of coming into a new country. When you see the *I* at the beginning of *immigration,* think of the word *in.* Keep our strategy in mind when you examine news reports, video clips, and historical documents with your groups. Understanding these terms will help us in upcoming lessons as we investigate what happened to more than 1 million refugees who fled war-ravaged countries immediately following the Vietnam War."

Phase Two: Scaffold Learning, Goal Setting, and Self-Assessment Through Guided Practice

Your mission: Balance the level of challenge with the support your students need to gradually assume more responsibility for their own learning. Establish the crucial link between explaining to your students what they should understand and be able to do and preparing them for a performance of understanding where you will see them actually do it.

To achieve this mission,

- Provide a level of challenge that is slightly above what students can do on their own, supporting them with hints, cues, and suggestions to build competence and confidence. *Do I appropriately increase the levels of challenge during practice?*
- Fade your support as students become more competent to encourage and extend independence with specific concepts and skills. *Am I adjusting my instruction and feed-forward information according to evidence of where my students are in relation to the learning target and success criteria? As my students become more competent, am I fading my suggestions and increasing my feed-forward information about what they are doing well, so that they will do more of it?*
- Ask goal-directed questions that scaffold critical thinking about success criteria to help students create a "mind map" for reaching the learning target. *Are my questions open-ended, goal-directed, and focused on the learning target and success criteria? Am I encouraging my students to ask effective questions?*
- Teach content-specific strategies and reasoning processes that increase the range of strategies students can use during their performance of understanding. *Do I provide hints, cues, and strategies that my students can use to feed themselves forward with this content? Am I providing students with time to practice and monitor their use of the strategies?*
- Observe and respond to class, group, and individual needs. *Based on the evidence I am gathering, do I know which concepts my students get, almost get, and struggle with? Am I supporting students by providing structured suggestions and fully formed examples? Does student performance evidence convince me that they are ready for independent practice with this concept? If I ask several*

students what they are learning and how well they are learning it, can they use the language of the success criteria to respond?

- Help students set mastery goals by encouraging them to apply look-fors to understand what quality work looks like for today's lesson. *Are my students applying look-fors to become more skillful at self-monitoring and self-assessment? Am I encouraging students to commit to the goal by helping them learn the skills they will need to reach it?*

Example: Ms. Wolfe scaffolds the learning of her 2nd grade students as they learn how to round a number to the nearest 10, using a number line divided into 10 sections: "When we round a number to the nearest 10, we ask ourselves, 'Which 10 is closest?' Let's practice what we mean. Draw a house over number 0 and label it 'My House.' Draw another house over number 10 and label it 'Rick's House.' The rest of the numbers are the other houses on the street. If you are playing with Rick in front of house number 4, and you want to go to one of your houses to play, whose house is closer, yours or Rick's? How do you know? That's the same thinking we use when we round to the nearest 10: we ask ourselves which 10 is closer."

Ms. Wolfe gives students another number line that shows five intervals of 10 (0 to 10, 10 to 20, 20 to 30, 30 to 40, and 40 to 50). Between each number are 10 slash marks. She explains, "When we round to the nearest 10, we ask which 10 is closer. This is the thinking strategy we used to decide which house was closer. Now find 26 on the number line. What are you looking for to help you decide which 10 is closer? Turn to your learning partner and share the questions you should ask yourself to decide how to round 26 to the nearest 10. Your goal is to share the good thinking strategies we are using so that we can all make the correct decision."

Ms. Wolfe circulates as students respond. She notices and names what students are doing well to encourage them to keep doing it. Rather than having students merely shout out their answers, she walks students through more examples, pointing out the success criteria and asking students to use the criteria to explain how they rounded to the nearest 10. Once the evidence she collects convinces her that students understand the process, she increases the level of challenge: "Find number 35 on the number line. What makes this number different from the other numbers we've used? Is this an easy decision, or is there something about this number that makes it harder to decide? What questions do you have about rounding this number to the nearest 10?"

Everything Ms. Wolfe does helps her gather and use evidence to guide students' thinking and doing. Students' success with this content depends on their ability to make accurate, independent decisions. Ms. Wolfe's goal-directed language and questions guide students toward conceptual understanding and mastery goals rather than simple, "right answer" performance goals.

Phase Three: Engage Students in a Performance of Understanding

Your mission: Feed your students forward as they use their newly developed knowledge and skills in a slightly different or more challenging independent practice format during a public performance of understanding. Encourage students to gather evidence along with you about what they know and where they need to focus their self-improvement efforts.

> **To achieve this mission,**
>
> - Explain to students that the task or activity will help them try on the learning target, deepen their understanding of important concepts and skills, and make their thinking visible so that they can gather evidence of what they know and how well they know it. *How can I provide feedback that tells students both how well they are doing and how they might do better?*
> - Encourage students to use look-fors to monitor the quality of their work as they are working. *Did I observe students assessing themselves? How can I use my feedback to encourage more self-assessment?*
> - Gather evidence with your students by asking them to supply reasons for the decisions they make. *Have my students met our success criteria for today's learning target? Can students justify their actions and reasoning by referring to the success criteria? How can I use the evidence I gathered to shape the level of challenge in tomorrow's lesson?*
> - Identify areas of strength and confusion, common questions, and issues that you want to address in your feedback. *What does the evidence from this performance tell me about the effectiveness of my teaching? What did I teach well, and what did I not teach so well?*

Example: During guided practice, Ms. Germani and her 8th grade students distinguished fact from opinion in written articles and blogs. Her feed-forward information scaffolded students' learning as they categorized selected statements and explained the reasons for their choices. Confident that her students are able to apply their new learning to a slightly more challenging task, Ms. Germani asks them to work individually to analyze a longer piece of writing that combines facts and opinions.

She directs students to select specific sentences, label each as either fact or opinion, and justify their decisions. She reminds students to apply their look-fors to identify the persuasive techniques that writers use to frame unsubstantiated statements as provable truths. She reminds students about the specific strategies they can use to avoid being misled by persuasive ploys. As students work, Ms. Germani circulates and acts as a cognitive coach, asking questions that incorporate look-fors to pull student thinking forward: "What convinces you that this statement is factual? Are statements that contain numbers and statistics always facts? What is your reason for describing this statement as inflammatory? Can a statement contain both factual information and speculation?"

Ms. Germani encourages students to monitor and assess their level of understanding: "Are you staying unbiased or letting your emotions influence you? Remember, writers intentionally provoke emotional reactions to sway you."

Ms. Germani notes what students are doing well, where they seem confused, and what she needs to reteach and to whom. Finally, she concludes the performance of understanding: "Review what you did and use our rubric to assess your work. What did you do well? Where did you have trouble? What do you need to learn more about, so that you are better able to separate facts from opinions?"

Phase Four: Provide Formative Feedback

Your mission: Provide students with descriptive information about what they did well. Then provide suggestions for exactly what they should do next to increase their understanding and skill and improve the quality of their work.

To achieve this mission,

- Use the language of the success criteria to describe exactly what students did well and why it is important to do more of it. *How can I use my feedback to make learning progress visible—to name exactly what students did well according the success criteria, and identify where they can improve?*
- To make students' learning visible, describe the reasoning and self-regulation skills that contributed to their success. *How can I draw attention to self-monitoring processes and self-assessment strategies that contribute to understanding?*
- Ask students to compare their self-assessment with your feedback. *How can showing and explaining examples of good work help students focus on important aspects of their own work?*

- Describe one or two specific areas where students can improve. *From the evidence I am gathering, what seem to be the logical next steps that certain students and groups of students should take to improve?*
- Explain and model specific strategies that students can use to increase their understanding and skill. *What content-specific or reasoning process–specific strategies can I provide to fine-tune students' understanding and skill and pull their thinking forward?*
- Provide targeted feedback to groups of students and individual students who need increased support to succeed. *How did the performance of understanding inform my decisions about differentiating my feed-forward information? How can it help me differentiate learning in tomorrow's lesson?*

Example: During their performance of understanding, students in Mr. Natale's 2nd grade class compared the characteristics of two different pieces of fruit. The performance demonstrated students' ability to use the comparison process they worked on during guided practice. Mr. Natale says, "We are becoming experts at the comparison process. You thoughtfully selected two pieces of fruit you wanted to compare. Everyone made good decisions for this first step. I noticed that the second step, naming the five things about the fruit that you wanted to compare, was a bit more challenging, and I saw you use your comparison strategies to work through it. Why is it important to state exactly what you want to compare before you move to the next step of saying how the two things are the same and how they are different? To get better at this step, make your descriptions of what you will compare more exact. For example, if you choose an apple and an orange, one of the things you can compare is taste. How could you make that comparison even more exact? One way is to think of the different ways to describe taste. So we could compare their sweetness. How would that make your comparison more exact? What could we say to make a more exact comparison between the size of an apple and the size of a pear?"

Mr. Natale breaks students into groups and asks them to work together to come up with five ways to compare a lemon and a lime using their new strategy of being more exact. He sits with a group of students who need more fully formed examples and strategies to overcome their struggles with the concept.

Phase Five: Give Students the Opportunity to Use the Feedback to Improve their Performance

Your mission: Maximize and gauge the effect of your feedback. Give students the golden second chance—the opportunity to attempt part of the performance again, this time informed by your feedback. This second chance benefits both halves of the classroom learning team: you will be able to gauge the effect of your feedback, and students will be able to improve their learning. Remember that feedback isn't effective unless students recognize it as such and can use it to improve their work (Brookhart, 2008; Moss & Brookhart, 2009).

To achieve this mission,

- Consider what students did well and what you suggested they do next to improve. *How can I give students the chance to face a slightly more challenging task to pull their understanding further forward?*
- Give students a specifically designed task that requires them to "do it again" using your feed-forward strategy to fine-tune or redirect their work. *What must I ask my students to do differently to master the important skills and content in today's learning target?*
- Stay in the "cognitive coach" mode by using feed-forward information to encourage self-monitoring, self-assessment, and goal setting as students engage in the task. *How can I increase students' ability to apply success criteria?*
- Gather evidence that you can use to point students toward success in tomorrow's lesson. *How will the task I assign help us gather additional evidence about student competence with this learning target to inform the appropriate level of challenge in tomorrow's lesson?*

Example: Mr. Natale listens to the groups as they describe the specific characteristics they used to compare a lemon and a lime during the performance of understanding. He comments on what happened in the groups: "Even though limes and lemons are very similar, they are also very different. Skin smoothness is a specific characteristic. Choosing to compare the smoothness of the lime's skin with the smoothness of the lemon's skin gives you an exact way to describe details that make the fruits alike and different."

He asks students to close their eyes and feel the skins of both fruits, then to open their eyes: "Look at their skins. Which is shinier? Does that give you another clue about their smoothness in addition to what you discovered when you felt their skins? We are showing that we can be detailed and that we are mastering the reasoning process of comparison. Now that we have that ability, let's do one more. In your groups, come up with three specific characteristics that you could use to compare a rose with a daisy."

LOOKING FORWARD

Using learning targets that focus on what progress looks like for today's lesson yields feedback that feeds learning forward, engages students as stakeholders in their own success, and prepares both halves of the classroom learning team for the increased level of challenge that will meet them tomorrow. Without a learning target, feedback is just someone telling you what to do!

Feeding students forward to become accomplished goal setters and confident, self-regulated learners has a tremendous effect on their achievement. To realize the full impact of the learning target theory of action, however, we must truly put students in the driver's seat. We can do this by helping them become assessment-capable—that is, by fostering the *skill* and the *will* to examine the quality of their own understanding and make strategic decisions about how to improve.

5

DEVELOPING ASSESSMENT-CAPABLE STUDENTS

Students are the most important decision makers in the classroom. A teacher might have wonderful learning intentions, garner lots of materials, and offer great instructional activities. But unless the student engages with these, very little learning occurs. To engage in learning, students need answers to the three central questions of the formative assessment process: Where am I going? Where am I now? How can I close the gap between where I am now and where I want to go?

Learning targets are the key to developing *assessment-capable students*—that is, students who regulate their own learning by answering these three questions as they work. It's the teacher's job to increase the *skill* (the ability to self-assess) and the *will* (the disposition to self-assess) of the most important data-driven decision makers of all: the students.

RESEARCH ON THE EFFECTS OF STUDENT SELF-ASSESSMENT

When teachers present to their classes a view of learning from *students'* perspective, they develop students' ability to regulate their own learning. Developing assessment-capable students who know the learning target for the lesson, can describe where they are in relation to the criteria for success, and can use that information to select learning strategies to improve their work is the number-one factor for improving student achievement (Hattie, 2009).

This perspective is a relatively recent development in education and may require a shift in thinking for some teachers. Back when learning theorists were behaviorists and teachers were taught to write behavioral objectives, instruction was conceived as the "stimulus" to which students "responded." The theory was that if the lessons were well constructed, students would learn as they participated in the lesson activities.

We now know that learning is an active process and that students are the agents of their own learning (Ormrod, 2009). Good self-assessment requires students to have a clear concept of the learning goals and criteria for success, to be able to recognize these characteristics in their own work, and to be able to translate their self-assessments into action plans for improvement. Numerous studies of student self-assessment demonstrate its value. A study of 3rd and 4th grade essay writing showed greater achievement for students who self-assessed using target criteria than for a comparison group of students who engaged in general self-reflection (Andrade, Du, & Wang, 2008). A study of 3rd graders' knowledge of multiplication facts showed not only achievement of the rote learning but also an understanding and enjoyment of self-assessment itself (Brookhart, Andolina, Zusa, & Furman, 2004).

Even young children can be involved in generating assessment criteria and using them for self-assessment. Higgins, Harris, and Kuehn (1994) studied 1st and 2nd grade students' generation of assessment criteria and their use of those criteria for self-assessment on group projects. At first, the children focused on group behavior and on neatness and other surface-level criteria. By the end of the year, however, they could identify substantive criteria as well. Brown (2008) developed a strategy called "Quick Check" that had 2nd graders use a self-assessment rubric. These students became more engaged as they recognized their progress, and their judgment improved over time, especially in terms of quality-oriented judgments (as opposed to quantity-oriented judgments like counting elements present in the work).

Several studies of self-assessment have been conducted at the secondary level as well. Ross, Hogaboam-Gray, and Rolheiser (2002) found an increase in problem-solving skills among 5th and 6th graders who received 12 weeks of self-evaluation training in mathematics. Andrade, Du, and Mycek (2010) found that 5th through 7th graders who used self-assessment on the basis of clear targets (model essays and a rubric) wrote better persuasive essays than did students in a comparison group who engaged in general self-reflection. And Ross and Starling (2008) studied student self-assessment using target criteria in 9th grade geography. Learning targets focused on students' ability to solve geography problems with global information system (GIS) software and explain their problem-solving strategies. The self-assessment group outscored a comparison group of students who did not self-assess on three different measures: the task of creating a map using the GIS software, a test measuring knowledge of the software, and—the largest difference—a report explaining their problem-solving strategies.

The ability to use self-assessment information to regulate one's own learning and behavior is a strong predictor of future academic and professional success (Bandura, 2008; Ormrod, 2011b). The good news is that self-assessment and self-regulation skills can be learned.

THREE GUIDING QUESTIONS AND THE FORMATIVE ASSESSMENT PROCESS

Most researchers and professional developers (Brookhart, 2010a; Chappuis & Chappuis, 2008; Educational Testing Service, 2009; Hattie & Timperley, 2007; Heritage, 2010; Sadler, 1989) center their work with teachers on the questions we have already described:

- Where am I going?
- Where am I now?
- How can I close the gap between where I am now and where I want to go?

These questions guide the formative assessment process and focus everything that happens in the classroom: what the teacher does, what the students do, and what the teacher and students do together.

Most important, students who become skilled at using this process "learn how to learn" (James et al., 2006). It all starts with students understanding where they are going—their learning target. In this chapter, we focus on student goal setting and self-assessment, processes that depend on students' understanding of both the target and the process of working toward it.

USING A FORMATIVE LEARNING CYCLE TO DEVELOP ASSESSMENT-CAPABLE STUDENTS

When classroom lessons consist of do-or-die tasks or assignments—one-time-only chances to demonstrate mastery—students have little chance or reason to learn how to assess their own work and to value the process. In sharp contrast, the formative learning cycle teaches and encourages students to improve their work as part of today's lesson. A basic formative learning cycle (see Figure 1.6 on p. 22) begins when the teacher models and explains the lesson's learning target and criteria for success—where students are headed in the lesson, how they will know when they get there, and how they will demonstrate their learning.

After the teacher explains the learning target, the students engage in guided practice, with the teacher scaffolding students' understanding of the success criteria and their ability to use the criteria to gauge the quality of their work. Next, students engage in the performance of understanding without teacher guidance, trying out their new learning to see where they are in relation to the success criteria. Immediately following students' independent performance, the teacher provides formative feedback to help them accurately assess what they did well and what they should do to improve their performance. The teacher's feedback also helps students select a strategy to use on their next attempt. Then students are given a chance to perform again, informed by new strategies and mindful of what they need to do to approach mastery of the learning target.

This informed second chance yields powerful motivational factors that strengthen students' views of themselves as assessment-capable. Whereas do-or-die assignments say to students, "This is how well you will ever do this" and promote a low sense of self-efficacy, teaching students to self-assess and use the information they gather to improve their subsequent work fosters a belief in their own ability to succeed. Students begin to understand mastery as a progressive learning process that is under their control and become optimistic about their ability to think and behave in increasingly intelligent ways (Cornoldi, 2010; Ormrod, 2011b).

USING LEARNING TARGETS TO SUPPORT STUDENT SELF-ASSESSMENT

In our professional development work with teachers and principals across the United States, we encourage them to apply a simple litmus test to gauge what is happening in their classrooms. Every student should be able to answer these two questions for today's lesson: "What am I learning [the learning target]? How will I know when I've learned it [the success criteria]?" And every teacher should be able to answer the parallel set of questions: "What is important for my students to learn and be able to do in this lesson? How will I know whether they've learned it?"

In this section, we present some strategies that scaffold student self-assessment at each stage in the formative assessment process. We also encourage you to design your own tools and strategies for the range of students and learning targets you teach.

Where Am I Going?

When many people hear the term *self-assessment,* they envision students assessing the quality of *current* work ("Where am I now?"). But sowing the seeds of self-assessment begins right at the beginning, with sharing the learning target and criteria for success. It is therefore crucial to share learning targets in a way that supports student self-assessment. Here are several strategies that will help.

HELP STUDENTS ENVISION SUCCESS CRITERIA BY ORGANIZING THEM AS STUDENT-FRIENDLY RUBRICS, CHECKLISTS, OR DISPLAYS. When students have a hand in creating rubrics, they develop a deeper understanding of them. For learning targets in which students already have some experience—for example, writing a report—students can co-create the rubrics. For learning targets in which students have very little experience, students can put teacher-made rubrics into their own words. These activities familiarize students more deeply with the criteria and help them understand what to look for in their own work.

PROVIDE EXAMPLES OF WORK AT ALL LEVELS AND TIME FOR STUDENTS TO SORT EXAMPLES BY SUCCESS CRITERIA. Students can take the rubrics they have organized or co-created and apply them to examples of work at different levels. This activity is good practice for later applying the rubrics to their own work.

USE GOAL-DIRECTED LANGUAGE TO EXPLAIN HOW LEARNING SUCCESS IN TODAY'S LESSON FITS INTO THE LEARNING TRAJECTORY. Students need to conceptualize the learning target as something to aim for. That makes a whole lot of sense if the students understand that the lesson really is going somewhere. For example, a teacher might say, "Today we are learning to read the symbols on a weather map. This is important, because weather maps can help us predict weather. By the end of the week, we should be able to use the weather maps in the newspaper or on the Internet to predict our own weather and the weather in parts of the country where we have friends and relatives." The learning target becomes a mini-goal for the lesson that constitutes one more step on the way to students' longer-term learning goals.

Where Am I Now?

When you have shared the learning target and criteria for success, assessing the current quality of work follows naturally. In other words, once students know where they are headed, they will want to know, "Are we there yet?"

Different learning targets need different performances of understanding and, therefore, different self-assessment strategies. The following sections should help you develop a repertoire of self-assessment strategies for students based on the kind of learning target involved.

FOR LEARNING TARGETS INVOLVING CONCEPTS, USE SELF-REFLECTION STRATEGIES OR INDICATOR SYSTEMS. Self-reflection sheets usually state a goal for students (or ask them to state it) and have them reflect on the quality of their work on one or more performances of understanding. Figure 5.1 gives an example of a self-reflection sheet for one assignment. Students identify the performance of understanding (the assignment) at the top and then reflect on their strengths and weaknesses. Teachers can use the weightlifting imagery as a way to help students talk about how they developed their strengths and decide what "exercises" they should do to improve their weaknesses.

By *indicator systems,* we mean "traffic light" color-coding, happy/sad faces, or any other coding system through which students can indicate their level of confidence in their work or their level of understanding of the concepts they are working with. Individual students can use indicator systems on their own work—for example, putting a green sticker on an assignment they have reviewed and decided they understood and succeeded on, a red sticker on an assignment they have decided is of poor quality but do not know how to improve, and a yellow sticker on an assignment they are not sure about. Grimes and Stevens (2009) teach 4th grade students to self-assess using the metaphor of an automobile windshield: the indicator categories are "glass" (I can see clearly), "bug" (I can see partly), and "mud" (I can't see anything).

These indicator systems help students in two ways. First, students' self-reflection itself furthers their awareness of the learning target and their work in relation to it. Second, they help students see where their next steps should occur. The symbols also enable teachers to give appropriate, helpful feedback focused on student-identified needs.

Whole classes can also use indicator systems for simultaneous self-assessment that the teacher can observe with a visual sweep of the classroom. For learning targets involving simple concepts or problems, students can "vote" the answers to questions by responding to a question with a thumbs-up or thumbs-down or other hand signals (for example, holding up one to five fingers to indicate a level of understanding from "none" to "complete"). Younger children can move more dramatically (for example, "Stand up if you think oil and water will mix when we stir them together"). For multiple-choice questions, students can hold up response cards with letters (*A, B, C,* or *D*) or use electronic response systems ("clickers"). Students can answer short constructed-response questions (for example, writing simple sentences or solving simple math problems) on whiteboards.

5.1 A Tool for Self-Reflection on One Assignment

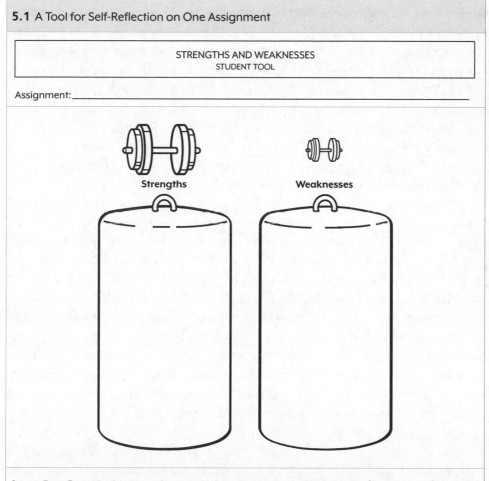

STRENGTHS AND WEAKNESSES
STUDENT TOOL

Assignment: _____

Strengths   Weaknesses

Source: From *Formative Assessment Strategies for Every Classroom: An ASCD Action Tool* (2nd ed., p. 248), by S. M. Brookhart, 2010, Alexandria, VA: ASCD. © 2010 by ASCD. Used with permission.

FOR LEARNING TARGETS INVOLVING WRITING, USE SELF-REFLECTION AND SELF- OR PEER-EDITING. The writing process is a classic example of the formative learning cycle. Each stage—prewriting, drafting, revising, proofreading, and publishing—provides an opportunity to self-evaluate and decide on strategies for improvement. Similarly, for any performance of understanding that asks students to write something over time—a report, for example—you can build in self- or peer-editing opportunities along the way.

FOR LEARNING TARGETS INVOLVING FACTS, USE TRACKING METHODS. Students can use graphs or charts to keep track of their progress toward learning targets involving facts, such as mathematical facts, vocabulary words, lists of states and capitals, or elements and their properties. For example, they might use a line graph or bar graph to display their scores on weekly math quizzes. After students make each entry in the graph, ask them whether they were satisfied with their performance—if so, elaborating on how they accomplished it, and if not, what they plan to do differently before the next quiz. Use these graphs carefully; when used indiscriminately, they can imply to students that the score matters more than the learning.

Another type of tracking method is a category system, which helps students learn by categorizing and grouping facts. For example, a student might print her 8-times facts on index cards and file each in a recipe box under one of three tabs—"fast," "slow," and "not yet"—to assess which answers she can give quickly (fast), which ones she doesn't know quite as well (slow), and which ones she cannot yet answer (not yet). She refiles the cards as they all make their way toward the "fast" category.

FOR LEARNING TARGETS INVOLVING CONTENT FROM SUBJECT-AREA TEXTBOOKS, USE SUMMARIZING AND SELF-TESTING METHODS. Students can summarize reading in their own words and evaluate how confident they are that they have understood the main points and details. Suggest that they discuss their summaries with peers. Students can also write their own lists of factual and inferential questions based on the text and try to answer them. They can also list vocabulary and concepts that they believe they understand as well as words and ideas they find difficult. All of these methods engage students in processing the material, not just memorizing it.

FOR LEARNING TARGETS INVOLVING COMPLEX PERFORMANCES, USE SELF-ASSESSMENT WITH RUBRICS. Complex performances require students to demonstrate more than one learning target. For example, students might solve a problem and explain their reasoning. Or they might prepare a report on a historical event, using research, historical analysis, and writing skills. Complex performances are good occasions to use co-created or student-transcribed rubrics on examples of work across a range of quality levels and then on students' own work.

One way to do this is to have students use highlighters with rubrics. To use this method, students *must* have a clear understanding of the learning target. To compare their work against a rubric, students need to read and understand the performance descriptions for all the levels of each criterion. Only then can students accurately highlight key phrases in the rubric from the level that they think describes their work. As their "evidence," they can use the same-color highlighter to mark elements of the writing in their drafts that show they have met the highlighted standard. For example, if a student highlighted "clearly states an opinion" in a rubric for a persuasive essay, that student would highlight his or her opinion in the draft in the same color (Andrade, Du, & Wang, 2008). Using a different color of highlighter in the rubric, students can identify any quality criterion that they do not believe their work met. These "other color" descriptions become qualities that the student will aim to develop next in the work.

Figure 5.2 (p. 88) provides examples of how teachers can organize learning targets and success criteria as a metacognitive tool to promote student self-assessment, goal setting, and self-regulation. Teachers and students can use the framework separately and then engage in formative conversations about students' growing competence.

DISCUSS THE ACCURACY AND FAIRNESS OF STUDENT SELF-ASSESSMENTS BY COMPARING THEM AGAINST SUCCESS CRITERIA. Self-assessments using rubrics or other tools are even more effective when they become vehicles for student-teacher discussion on the accuracy of students' self-judgments. Teach students to self-assess accurately by working on two different aspects of student self-judgment. First, make sure students truly understand the learning target and the success criteria; students can be accurate judges of the quality of their work only to the extent that they understand the learning target and success criteria deeply, and only when they share a similar understanding of quality with their teacher (Sadler, 1989). Second, recognize that some students will look at their work through "rose-colored glasses," evaluating it as they wish it to be, not as it actually is, while other students will just rush through the self-evaluation without thinking much about it. Providing feedback on the accuracy and fairness of their self-assessments is the best way to strengthen students' self-assessment skills.

5.2 Three Examples of Learning Targets and Success Criteria Organized as a Metacognitive Tool

High School Example

Learning target: *Use information from maps, charts, and graphs to identify distinguishing factors of different Western European countries.*

This means I can:	Not yet	On my way	Got this
• Use maps to compare and contrast different landforms.			
• Create a graph that compares the average wealth of citizens of three Western European countries.			
• Map the natural resources of the Western European countries.			

Rate your mastery of the learning target. Remember your rating can change over time. → → → → →

Middle School Example

Learning target: *Explain how maps provide information about direction, location, and distance.*

This means I can:	Not yet	On my way	Got this
• Draw a map of the playground and label north, south, east, and west.			
• Use a map of our school to give directions from the cafeteria to the principal's office using the phrases *right turn* and *left turn*.			
• Create a key for my playground map with symbols for swings, slides, and the baseball diamond.			

Mark where you are on your way to the learning target. Then select a strategy you will use to improve. → → → → →

Elementary School Example

Learning target: *Follow a treasure map to a hidden bag of pennies in my classroom.*

This means I can:	Not yet	On my way	Got this
• Follow the "paces" on the treasure map by counting my steps.			
• Demonstrate two paces north and then four paces east.			
• Use the treasure map to give one set of directions (walk two paces north) to my group's "treasure hunter."			

Here is where I am on my way to my learning target. I can watch myself learn and grow. → → → → →

PROVIDE DESCRIPTIVE, NONJUDGMENTAL FEEDBACK THAT MODELS ACCURATE ASSESSMENT OF STUDENT STRENGTHS AND NEEDS BY FAIRLY COMPARING THE STUDENT'S WORK AGAINST THE SUCCESS CRITERIA. Students learn how to evaluate their work against criteria by watching their teachers model the process, by talking about it, and by seeing the difference it can make in the eventual quality of their work. For your part, model accurate assessment and fair comparison against the criteria, then provide an immediate opportunity for students to use that feedback and observe the results. These strategies contribute to a learning culture in the classroom by demonstrating that teacher feedback and student self-assessment are two sides of the same coin, that both are "safe," and that both contribute to learning.

How Can I Close the Gap Between Where I Am Now and Where I Want to Go?

Self-assessing without making an action plan for improvement is like reading a recipe without actually preparing the dish: it's nice to think about, but it doesn't help get dinner on the table. Helping students identify their next learning move and follow through with it is potentially the most important step in the self-assessment process.

HELP STUDENTS SET REALISTIC AND ACCURATE GOALS BY COMPARING THEIR WORK AGAINST THE SUCCESS CRITERIA. Frame rubrics as maps to success by sharing them with students before the lesson, using their language to explain the lesson, and helping students apply the rubrics' criteria to drafts of their work. Realistic goals can be derived from rubrics' performance-level descriptions. If a student's work is at level 2 on a rubric, for example, an obvious goal would be to raise his or her performance to level 3. That's a performance goal, not a learning goal, but if the rubric is well constructed, the student can *make* the performance goal a learning goal by using the performance-level description associated with performance at level 3. For some learning targets, the performance of understanding can be literally tracked as rings on a target (see Figure 5.3, p. 90).

Alternatively, consider providing students with a list of possible mastery goals, each tied to a specific part of the success criteria. A student may be working at a proficient level on ideas for writing but be below proficient in using standard grammar conventions, for example. This student would aim for developing more creative, advanced writing ideas and using grammar more proficiently.

5.3 A Tool for Helping Students Track Progress Toward a Learning Target

Hit the Target

Look at your work on:_____

Place a dot on the target and the date you made that "hit."

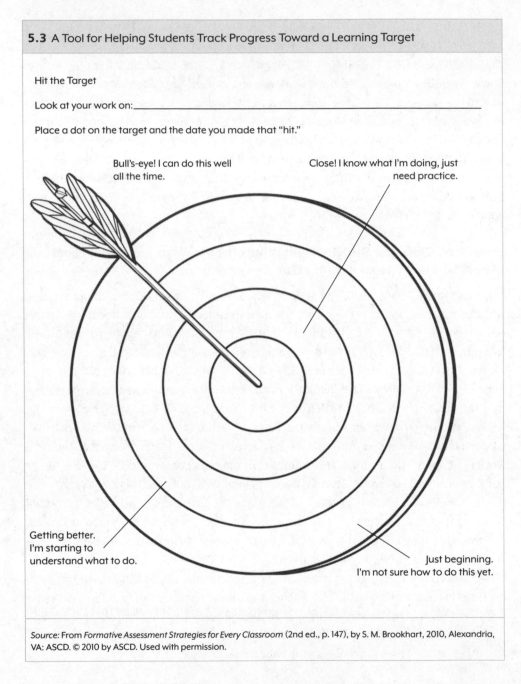

Bull's-eye! I can do this well all the time.

Close! I know what I'm doing, just need practice.

Getting better. I'm starting to understand what to do.

Just beginning. I'm not sure how to do this yet.

TEACH TARGETED LEARNING STRATEGIES AS AN INTEGRAL PART OF THE LESSON. Elementary-level reading teachers are used to teaching reading strategies, regularly asking their students to do things like sound out words, use finger tracking or a bookmark to focus their eyes, and use context clues. Similarly, mathematics teachers teach problem-solving strategies, regularly asking their students to identify the nature of the problem (e.g., "Does the problem ask you to put things together? Then use addition."), identify the relevant numbers, write the problem as an equation, and so on.

You should give students strategies for doing *every* lesson, in all subjects and at all grade levels. Some students can figure out strategies on their own. But if you provide strategies, you give *all* students methods for approaching their work. Suggest a strategy ("Here's how I might go about doing this assignment . . .") and then ask other students to share how they might approach the work. A brief discussion of this nature gets students to share, provides all students with a variety of suggestions about how to work, and—most important—communicates to students that they should be active and strategic learners who are continually figuring out how to learn.

PROVIDE FEEDBACK THAT IDENTIFIES A STRATEGY FOR GROWTH LINKED TO THE SUCCESS CRITERIA, AND GIVE STUDENTS A CHANCE TO USE THE FEEDBACK TO IMPROVE. In addition to providing descriptions of where students are now and a description of where they need to go next, teachers should suggest strategies that students can use to get to where they need to go.

Let's look at a classroom example. History teachers often address how civilizations met their needs based on their specific constraints. For example, various cultures had to solve the problem of preserving food. In addition to unpacking the historical concepts in a lesson on how people in ancient Mesopotamia used salt to preserve their food, the teacher can teach problem-solving strategies that extend students' ability to grapple with upcoming historical concepts. A discussion of how decisions are bound and informed by limiting conditions as well as needs would help students figure out how to learn history by applying specific reasoning strategies.

As the teacher walks students through the content example, he can point out the specific constraint and ask students to use an unstructured problem-solving model, then suggest a strategy for growth focused by the idea of "Where am I now?": "We learned how these ancient people used salt to preserve their food so that they could store it at room temperature. As we move into a study of the Incas, a culture that learned to store three to seven years' worth of food, we can apply a simple problem-solving model to learn about their culture. These questions outline the steps that will help us: What was the food preservation goal they were aiming for, and why? What were their limiting conditions? How did they overcome their constraints? How can we evaluate the effectiveness of their decisions?"

SCAFFOLD SELF-ASSESSMENT SKILLS IN ALL LEARNERS

All students can and should learn how to self-assess—to observe themselves and adapt what they are doing as a means to improve their work and understand their growing competence over time. It's true that some high-achieving students may have better self-assessment and self-regulation skills than students who are struggling, but it's dangerous to assume that all high-achieving students consistently and effectively self-assess. Some students may have done well because the curriculum wasn't challenging. It is just as dangerous to assume that young learners or students with learning challenges lack what it takes to assess their own work and take steps to improve it.

As with any concept or skill, different students have different strengths and needs when it comes to accurately assessing their own work and using that information to regulate what they do to improve it. Scaffolding any new skill requires that we provide incremental challenge and support as we pull our students to higher levels of competence. Figure 5.4 illustrates how teachers can enhance student self-assessment by adjusting their level of support in accordance with each student's growing competence.

LOOKING FORWARD

Learning targets and criteria for success increase student agency by showing students where they are headed with their learning. Students can't assess themselves effectively unless they have a goal in mind and understand what it looks like. When they *do* have a goal in mind and understand what it looks like, self-assessment becomes the obvious next step: Am I getting there? What else do I need to do?

In short, learning targets are the foundation of student self-assessment. They are also the foundation of differentiated instruction, which we turn to in Chapter 6.

5.4 Strategies to Challenge and Support Self-Assessment Growth

Self-Assessment Skill Building Block *I can…*	Continuum of Competence Strategies		
	Learn/Practice	Gain Competence	Enhance/Extend
Describe success criteria for today's lesson.	The teacher shares the success criteria in student-friendly language to explain what good work looks like for the lesson.	The student explains and paraphrases the success criteria in his or her own language.	The student generates success criteria for a specific product or performance.
Apply the success criteria to my work.	The teacher teaches, demonstrates, and guides students in applying the success criteria to exemplars representing different levels of quality.	The teacher guides the student in applying the success criteria to his or her own work to identify one area of strength and one area of need.	The student applies multiple success criteria to complex products or performances.
Determine the accuracy and fairness of my self-assessment.	The teacher provides feedback on how well the student's assessment focused on a factor specified in the success criteria.	The student compares his or her self-assessment with the teacher's assessment on several success criteria; they discuss areas of agreement and disagreement.	The student works with peers to discuss self-assessment for a complex product or performance.
Set a goal for improvement.	The teacher provides an appropriate goal for the student.	The teacher provides a list of mastery goals, and the student chooses a goal based on his or her own self-assessment.	The student uses self-assessment information to determine a mastery goal or set of goals appropriate to the success criteria and the performance of understanding.
Select a strategy to improve my work using the success criteria.	The teacher provides a specific strategy for producing good work and describes it using the success criteria.	The teacher provides a list of next-step improvement strategies, and the student chooses a strategy based on his or her own self-assessment.	The student selects, adapts, or designs a learning strategy based on his or her informed goals for improvement.

USING LEARNING TARGETS TO DIFFERENTIATE INSTRUCTION

Differentiating instruction is the process of matching students' needs to the requirements for achievement. Differentiated instruction recognizes "students' varying background knowledge, readiness, language, preferences in learning, and interests" (Hall, Strangman, & Meyer, 2011, p. 3) and provides "different avenues to acquiring content, to processing or making sense of ideas, and to developing products so that each student can learn effectively" (Tomlinson, 2001, p. 1). In other words, differentiating instruction helps all students reach their learning targets.

Two widely used models for differentiated instruction are Tomlinson's (2001, 2003) model for Differentiated Instruction (DI) and Hall, Strangman, and Meyer's (2011) principles of Universal Design for Learning (UDL). DI arose in the general education context and emphasizes differentiating goals, materials, instruction, and assessment for all students. UDL arose in the special education context and emphasizes minimizing barriers to goals, materials, instruction, and assessment for all students. They end up, as you can see, in a similar place. Figure 6.1 outlines the two models next to each other.

6.1 Two Models for Differentiating Instruction

The Model	How the Model Meets Diverse Student Needs	What Students Are Learning	Methods Used by the Model
Differentiated Instruction (DI)	Student elements of the DI model: • Readiness. • Interest. • Learning profile. • Affect. (Tomlinson, 2003)	State standards and benchmarks Local curriculum goals and objectives	Classroom elements of the DI model: • Content. • Process. • Product. • Learning environment. (Tomlinson, 2003)
Universal Design for Learning (UDL)	Minimize barriers and maximize flexibility. (Hall et al., 2011)	State standards and benchmarks Local curriculum goals and objectives	Principles of the UDL framework: • To support recognition of learning; provide multiple, flexible methods of presentation. • To support strategic learning; provide multiple, flexible methods of expression and apprenticeship. • To support affective learning; provide multiple, flexible options for engagement. (Hall et al., 2011)

We have heard at least three kinds of arguments mustered in support of the thesis that instruction should be differentiated for different learners. A practical argument makes the case that you can either deal with individual differences in instruction or live with individual differences in learning outcomes (Bloom, 1984; Guskey, 2007; Katz, 2009). A theoretical argument highlights differences in motivation, aptitude, prior learning, and background experience that lead to differences in learning needs (Hattie,

2009). A humanitarian argument makes the case for treating students as individuals, recognizing who they are, and helping them do their best (Dewey, 1900; Neill, 1960). All these arguments converge in support of differentiating instruction.

DECIDING WHEN AND HOW TO DIFFERENTIATE

Learning targets should help teachers decide how and when to differentiate instruction. In principle, we support giving students choice and variety whenever possible. However, there are degrees to which choice matters for learning. The choices that matter most lie in the ways we deliver content to students, the ways students engage with the content, and the ways students make the content their own. The more directly a differentiation strategy leads to the learning target, the more important it is for learning.

For example, consider two 8th grade teachers who are both teaching U.S. history. One learning goal for the unit is that the student "understands that specific individuals and the values those individuals held had an impact on history" (Kendall & Marzano, 2004). Each teacher explains that the current lesson's learning target is understanding George Washington's role in the birth of the United States as a nation. Each teacher assigns a project that asks, "Why was George Washington uniquely suited to become 'the father of our country'?" Realizing that students in their classes have different levels of background and interest in doing this topic, both teachers give students some choice in how they will approach the assignment.

Mr. Smith assigns students a conventional research paper. He tells students that George Washington was "the right man at the right time" to be a leader at a pivotal time in U.S. history and that he expects this assignment to help students discover how Washington's personal qualities, military background, values and beliefs, and political skill contributed to his role in U.S. history. Mr. Smith has requirements for the paper's length, number of sources, and format. He wants to diversify the experience for students of varying ability levels, so he gives students the option of doing a five-page report alone or a 10-page report with a partner, reasoning that a low-achieving student might benefit from working with a peer. In addition, students will get extra points in their grade if they dress up like George Washington on the day the paper is due.

Like Mr. Smith, Ms. Jones gives her students a research paper assignment and introduces George Washington as a unique figure in U.S. history. Ms. Jones also wants to diversify the experience for students of varying ability levels. Because her students have varied reading abilities, she gathers books and articles on many different reading levels. Her students also have varied writing abilities, so she varies the requirements for paper length and format for different students. All students, however, must make and support at least two different points in response to the research paper's question and substantiate their work with at least four different sources.

Let's examine how effectively the two teachers differentiated the assignment. Neither of the choices Mr. Smith offered was effective. One of the choices he built into his assignment was unrelated to the learning target: dressing up like George Washington doesn't help students learn about the importance of a unique figure in U.S. history. The other student choice Mr. Smith allowed, working with a partner, may or may not have been related to the learning target and was therefore dangerous because it let in the possibility of no learning happening. A partnership for a joint paper could be a good learning experience for both students, or it could be an exercise in letting one partner do all the work—and Mr. Smith will not know which it was. His well-intentioned differentiation will not necessarily lead to a classwide understanding of the influence of this historical figure.

In contrast, the differentiation Ms. Jones built into her assignment was central to the learning target. She provided resources at varying reading levels because reading was not primarily what she wanted students to learn. She varied the writing requirements for the paper because writing was not primarily what she wanted students to learn.

Interestingly, in our experience, teachers have less trouble with the idea of varying inputs (e.g., providing resources at varying reading levels) than with the idea of varying outputs (e.g., allowing students to write papers of different lengths). This trouble stems from a misconception about the meaning of the grade. Some teachers think the grade is what students *earn*. If that's true, then the "job" students do has to be the same. But a grade should really be an indicator of what students *learn*—and the students' task needs to be an indicator of what they were supposed to learn, too. In this case, reading difficult material and writing lengthy text were not part of what the teachers intended their students to learn—which was an understanding of the influence of people in history. Lack of reading and writing skills shouldn't get in the way of reaching the history learning target for students who, with simplified content, were quite capable of learning the concept Mr. Smith and Ms. Jones were trying to teach them.

FOCUSING DIFFERENTIATED INSTRUCTION WITH LEARNING TARGETS

The learning target is central to planning good differentiated instruction right from the beginning. It is the reference point toward which your observations and assessments of students' readiness, interest and affect, and learning profile need to point for you to plan effective instruction for that particular content or skill. The reason the learning target (the students'-eye view of the intentions for learning) is a better reference point than the instructional objective (the teacher's-eye view) is that students will need to help you get the right information. After all, it is the students who are ready or not, interested or not, and able or not to aim for the learning target. Figure 6.2 presents some strategic questions you can use to focus your assessments of students' needs on the learning target.

6.2 Strategic Questions for Assessing Student Elements to Plan for Differentiated Instruction

Element	Strategic Questions
Readiness	• Where is the student now in relation to the learning target? • What portions of the learning target has the student already mastered? • What lack of prior knowledge may be a barrier to achieving the learning target? • What supplemental skills (e.g., reading, writing, speaking, drawing) are necessary for students to hit this target, and where is the student in relation to those skills?
Interest and Affect	• How interested is the student in the content and the kinds of thinking and skills represented in the learning target? • What, if any, are the student's personal connections with the content and the kinds of thinking and skills represented in the learning target? • What prior experiences and feelings, if any, does the student have with the content and the kinds of thinking and skills represented in the learning target?
Learning Profile	• What are the student's preferences for accessing content (hear, see, read), learning activities, and modes of expression? • How do these preferences relate to the learning target?

READINESS. Planning for any instruction, differentiated or not, should begin with identifying the learning target and making a definite plan for how you're going to share it with students. Teachers can assess students' readiness using a variety of methods, formal or informal. A class discussion, for example, can serve the joint purposes of ascertaining readiness and activating prior knowledge. For some skills with definite prerequisites, like adding three-digit numbers, a short pre-test on the prerequisites (like adding two-digit numbers) can be helpful.

It's also important to assess readiness on supplemental skills. For example, research papers are a conventional method for teaching certain science or social studies standards. However, research papers require inquiry skills and writing skills that, while great skills to have, may not be the main point of doing the paper. If some students are likely to have trouble with the writing and therefore will not be able to learn the content, that's a good opportunity for differentiating the learning process so that students who can't read and write as well are not denied the opportunity to learn the content because of it.

INTEREST AND AFFECT. Assessment of student interest and affect is usually informal. Every once in a while, a more formal method might be useful—for example, having students construct, administer, and analyze a simple class survey in preparation for a lesson or unit. But usually, you can discern students' interests from talking with them and observing them. Use the questions like the ones in Figure 6.2 to ascertain students' interests and feelings toward the learning target.

Then, preferably with the students, identify springboards and barriers. Build into your lessons as many personal connections for students as you can, making them as central to the learning target as possible. For example, in a geometry lesson about right triangles, students interested in baseball might identify, measure, and calculate perimeter or area of all the right triangles they can find on a baseball field (e.g., from the pitcher's shoulder to the pitcher's feet to home plate). This assignment uses students' interests in a way more central to the learning target than, say, playing "math baseball" with the class, using a sheet of right-triangle problems as the pitches.

LEARNING PROFILE. When teachers understand students as learners, they are better able to give diverse learners access to learning targets. Do not confuse learning *profile* with learning *style*. The idea of measuring a student's learning style and then matching instruction to it has not held up under study (Doyle & Rutherford, 1984; Hyman & Rosoff, 1984; Scott, 2010). The assumption behind matching instruction to students' learning styles is that *teachers* are going to diagnose the student with some sort of "style" and then package content in that style for that student. In this conceptualization, the teacher does all the work.

Instead, focus on the learning target and the student's background, experience, and readiness for learning it. Consider, from the student's point of view, what concepts and skills need to be mastered (that is, the learning target). Help students understand what it is *they* are to learn, so *they* can aim for it, and help them identify aspects of themselves as learners that will help or hinder this process. If I, as a student, intend to learn about the rotation and revolution of the planets, and I know I have a hard time with spatial relationships unless I draw them, then I'd better get busy drawing. And if my teacher knows that, too, she can make sure drawing is part of my instruction.

Differentiating Instructional Planning

Figure 6.3 presents some strategies that you can use to center your planning for differentiated instruction on the learning target. The strategies are organized by the classroom elements in Tomlinson's (2003) DI model. However, they also contain UDL strategies to help teachers make curriculum "more broadly flexible and broadly supportive" (Hall et al., 2011, p. 9) for all learners. The sections below address each classroom element in more depth.

CONTENT. Differentiate content so that students can take different paths to the same learning target. Present a variety of examples that will resonate with different students—for example, you might use examples from both shopping and baseball for a learning target about per-unit calculations. Highlight features of the content that are crucial to the learning target, and show how they operate in all the examples. Use tiered methods to enable students of different ability levels (in relation to the specific learning target) to interact with the content in a meaningful way.

Here is a true story about a 7th grader named Dawson, who didn't seem to be able to learn much in language arts classes. He moved around a lot and talked in class more than his teacher would have liked, although not maliciously. One of his teacher's instructional goals was for students to learn how to spell 20 vocabulary words a week. Dawson routinely spelled about 3 of the words correctly each week. The reading support teacher suggested assigning Dawson just the first 10 words each week. His teacher followed this suggestion, but it did not make sense to her. To her mind, he was supposed to learn 20 words, just like his classmates, because 20 words was *her* instructional goal. She did not think in terms of a learning target for Dawson, who never did envision himself as someone who could competently spell 10 words a week,

6.3 Strategies for Differentiating Elements of Instruction

Element	Strategies
Content	• Present content using multiple examples, in different media and formats. • Highlight critical (to the learning target) features of the content. • Use tiered methods so that students of different ability levels (with regard to the learning target) can interact with the content meaningfully.
Process	• Provide diverse examples of skilled performance (different ways to hit the learning target). • Provide opportunities for students to practice with varying amounts of scaffolding. • Provide descriptive feedback. • View mistakes as opportunities for learning. • Have students keep track of their progress.
Product	• Keep all assignments substantive and related to the learning target. • Use the learning target to evaluate whether the (differentiated) products actually all help students accomplish and demonstrate the intended learning. • Use criterion-referenced evaluation for final products.
Learning Environment	• Offer choices in content, tools, and level of challenge (consistent with the learning target). • Offer choices of rewards and other affirmations. • Offer choices of work environment (consistent with the learning target). • Attribute success to effort, and the reason for effort to learning something new.

much less 20. We wonder what would have happened if the teacher had simply asked, "Dawson, how many of these words do you think you can learn to spell this week?"

PROCESS. One of the hallmarks of a differentiated classroom is a pattern of whole-class, small-group, and individual activities. Planning these activities effectively requires paying attention to the learning target—to what students are trying to achieve. Just implementing different types of activities is not in itself differentiating instruction; for example, group work that doesn't specify what each student should be accountable for learning is not effective (Johnson & Johnson, 2009; Kagan, 1989/1990). Most instructional activities are designed to help students interact with content (facts, concepts, principles, and generalizations) and use it to learn how to think and reason with it, build ideas with it, and relate it to other ideas.

Another hallmark of a differentiated classroom is flexible instructional activities that move students with different readiness levels, interests, and learning profiles toward their learning targets. Sometimes these take the form of *tiered assignments* (see Wormeli, 2006, especially Chapter 5), which tier the complexity and challenge of an assignment to accommodate students at varying levels of readiness. Other times these activities take the form of open-ended questions that can be answered in different ways by students at different readiness levels or with different interests or perspectives (Moss & Brookhart, 2009; Small, 2010).

Both the ways in which students engage with the content and the ways in which they express that engagement can be differentiated. Plan different ways for students to hit the learning target. For example, students can read about a topic and then write about it; they can watch a video and then draw something about it; and they can listen to a lecture about a topic and then talk about it themselves. All sorts of combinations are possible.

Plan performances of understanding that involve varying amounts of teacher help. For example, while the class is working on an assignment, you might pull the five students you see struggling the most into a small group to work with you at a table. Give descriptive feedback followed by opportunities to use the feedback, using the formative learning cycle. Feedback that is based on students' own work is by its nature differentiated.

PRODUCT. Learning targets are the key to keeping assignments substantive and avoiding what Wormeli (2006, p. 34) calls "fluff" assignments. The learning target is the gauge you use to evaluate whether the products actually help students accomplish and demonstrate the intended learning—that is, whether the assignment is truly a performance of understanding. We love Wormeli's concept of a fluff assignment, and our favorite is his entreaty to "please [never] hold an ancient Greece festival where all students learn is how to keep togas tied to their shoulders" (p. 35).

Some fluff assignments are done in the name of differentiated instruction. They give the concept a bad name, and they can actually keep students from learning. For example, consider a 6th grade math class. One of the Common Core State Standards in 6th grade geometry is

> Find the area of right triangles, other triangles, special quadrilaterals, and
> polygons by composing into rectangles or decomposing into triangles and

other shapes; apply these techniques in the context of solving real-world and mathematical problems.

The learning target for one lesson is to find the area of octagons. Students have been given the learning target "I can find the area of an octagon," coupled with a big picture of that classic octagon, a red stop sign, at the front of the class. They have been given the criteria for success as a little checklist:

> ☑ I can divide the octagon into triangles and rectangles.
> ☑ I can find the correct area of each triangle and rectangle.
> ☑ I can add all the little areas correctly and label the final area in square units.

The teacher decided that she would differentiate instruction for this lesson. Three of her 22 students were not yet ready to find the area of an octagon, and three others already knew how to do it. So while most of the class worked on octagon-area problems, the three "unready" students were given a hidden-picture puzzle in which they had to find and trace all the octagons in the picture. The three students who could already find the area of an octagon were given an extended exercise that had them draw their own irregular polygons, with at least eight sides, and find their areas.

The create-your-own-polygon assignment is a good example of a differentiated product. It extends the learning target, building on it in ways that enhance the general learning standard of knowing how to decompose shapes to find area and being able to solve problems using that concept.

The hidden-picture puzzle, on the other hand, was a fluff assignment. The teacher ascertained that students weren't ready and gave them an assignment that wouldn't help them get ready. Were the students unable to see how polygons can be divided up into smaller shapes? Did they not know how to find the area of triangles and rectangles? Were they unable to do the multiplication involved in the formulas? If the teacher had investigated *why* students weren't ready, she could have planned substantive instructional activities in the learning trajectory, with real learning targets of their own.

LEARNING ENVIRONMENT. To create a strong classroom environment, focus on helping all students access important learning targets (Ames & Archer, 1988). Offer choices in assignments that give students a chance to be self-regulated and feel in charge of their own learning—*but make sure the choices are consistent with the learning target*. For example, if a teacher gives students a choice of making a trifold display or using presentation software to share their findings from a science project about star and planet systems, that's nice—but it's not central to the learning target. In contrast, if the teacher gives students a choice about which star and planet system they will study, that *is* central to the learning target.

Help students see that it was their own efforts that led to success, and help them articulate how their understanding of the criteria for success led to their learning ("I practiced finding the area of polygons until I could do these problems easily and could explain my work").

Differentiating the Performance of Understanding and Criteria for Success

Many teacher education programs teach lesson planning according to a conventional model: the teacher first derives instructional objectives from unit goals, then plans instructional activities to teach those objectives, and finally administers an assessment to see how well students learned. There are lots of formats for this model, but they all follow the same general structure—and they all have teachers plan only what *they* are going to do.

We suggest an expanded model of planning that supports differentiated instruction and formative assessment. Not surprisingly, learning targets play a key role. Figure 6.4 presents the outline for this planning model.

Here is an example of how this model plays out in Mr. Jaworsky's 8th grade social studies unit. He starts with Montana Social Studies Content Standard 5, which also happens to be a curriculum goal in his district:

> Students make informed decisions based on an understanding of the economic principles of production, distribution, exchange, and consumption.

One of the benchmark performances for grade 8 is for students to

> Identify and explain basic economic concepts (e.g., supply, demand, production, exchange, and consumption; labor, wages, and capital; inflation and deflation; and private goods and services).

Mr. Jaworsky decides that this unit will focus on the concepts of supply, demand, production, exchange, and consumption. Students studied the concepts of labor, wages, and capital in a previous unit.

6.4 A Model of Instructional Planning to Support Student Engagement, Differentiated Instruction, and Formative Assessment

Start with a state standard(s) or curriculum goal(s).

1. What does the general standard or goal entail? Select one specific aspect of it that is the right grain size for a classroom unit.

2. List the lesson-sized learning targets that your students are going to pursue as they work to reach those learning goals, and the criteria for success.

   - Plan at least one lesson activity to communicate each learning target and its criteria for success to students.

   - Include in that activity ways for students to express their backgrounds, experiences, readiness, and interest regarding the learning target.

3. Brainstorm and list as many potential activities for instruction for each learning target as you can.

   - Have more than you would need for teaching.

   - Extras can help you diversify instruction (presenting content in multiple ways, providing different performances of understanding).

4. Brainstorm and list as many potential assessment methods to show performance on each learning target as you can.

   - Have more than you would need for grading.

   - Extras can be used for formative assessments (for practice, feedback, and coaching).

   - Extras can help you use multiple measures to more validly represent the domain and/or to diversify assessment methods.

5. Customize a general rubric for standards-based grading of student performance on this learning target. Decide how you would apply the rubric to each of the assessments you brainstormed. For example, for a test, what would be the cut points, and why? For a performance assessment, what would be the evidence for each level, and why?

Now at step 2 in the planning model, Mr. Jaworsky translates his instructional objectives for the unit into lesson-sized learning targets and criteria for success. For our purposes, we will examine just one of the learning targets for the unit. One of Mr. Jaworsky's instructional objectives is "Students comprehend the principle of supply and demand." Here are the learning target and criteria for success that he derives from this objective:

> I understand the principle of supply and demand. I will know I understand supply and demand when
>
> ☑ I can explain supply and demand in my own words.
> ☑ I can give examples of the principle of supply and demand in operation and examples of when the principle of supply and demand is not operating in our current economy.
> ☑ I can use the concept of supply and demand to make predictions about prices in the future.

Mr. Jaworsky plans a brief activity to share the learning target and criteria for success with students. He begins this introductory activity by asking two students to volunteer to come to the front of the class and participate in an impromptu skit. He tells them that the characters they are to play are two 6-year-old children. He shows the two students a toy (a nice shiny truck, perhaps) and tells them to act out a scenario in which they are two siblings who both want to play with the toy. Of course, they will fight over it. When this little scene is over, he produces another toy just like the first, gives one to each student, and tells them to act out the scenario again. This time, they will play together.

He then asks students to think about two questions:

- Why is gold expensive?
- Why is dirt cheap?

During the introductory activity, Mr. Jaworsky checks students' prior knowledge of and interest in the concept of supply and demand, which will allow him to differentiate instruction appropriately. He conducts this check using a quick think-pair-share activity around the questions "What do you know about the concepts of supply and demand?" and "What about those ideas most interests you?" Finally, he either gives students copies of the learning target and criteria for success or shows students their location on the chalkboard or bulletin board.

It has really taken us longer to write down this plan than it takes Mr. Jaworsky to execute it. The whole process takes about 10 minutes of class time. We wanted to write out this part of the planning process in some detail because the learning target and criteria for success are so important, as is the teacher's understanding of student background, readiness, and interest regarding the learning target. But we don't want you to get the idea that this planning process is lengthy. It's a brainstorming process.

Mr. Jaworsky is now at step 3 in the planning model depicted in Figure 6.4. He brainstorms a list of potential instructional activities for helping students understand the principle of supply and demand. He doesn't write complete instructions for all of the activities; at this stage, he is creating a library of strategies that he can use for the topic. He aims to have more ideas than he thinks he will need so that he can be flexible in his instruction. His ideas for instructional activities include a variety of methods of content presentation (e.g., print and other media, simulations and other experiences) and a variety of ways for students to process that content (e.g., reading, writing, graphing, talking, and researching). Here is Mr. Jaworsky's initial list of activity ideas:

- Read a chapter on supply and demand in a textbook.
- Watch a video on supply and demand.
- Look up "supply and demand" on Wikipedia.
- Participate in a class simulation game with scarce and plentiful goods, and then reflect on it.
- Simulate different supply-and-demand scenarios with graphs of supply-and-demand curves.
- Engage in group discussions on the question "What is the principle of supply and demand, and why should we care?" and report insights to the class.
- Conduct an Internet research project of looking up prices for various scarce and plentiful goods, and prepare a report.
- Come up with some popular, in-demand products, and find out as much as you can about their manufacture and distribution and how these have changed with the products' popularity and availability.

We want you to notice two things about this list. First, all the activities lead in some way toward an understanding of the principle of supply and demand. None of them are "fluff" activities. Second, because the activities incorporate multiple, flexible methods of presenting content and engaging students in processing that content, this list will be useful for differentiating instruction. For example, a student who doesn't read very well might find the video a good way to learn the concepts, whereas a student who is strong in mathematics might find playing with supply-and-demand curves the best way for her to understand the concepts. Students who learn well with others might find one of the group projects a good way to gain an understanding of the concepts.

To make these ideas live instructional activities, Mr. Jaworsky just needs to provide students with complete directions and access to the resources they will need. He starts by preparing the directions and resources for a subset of these activities to see how it goes. He already knows his students well enough to have in mind one activity he wants them all to do (watch the video) and several group projects that will serve as performances of understanding for different students, based on their needs and interests. As the lesson progresses—in this case, over several days—he will keep the extra activities waiting in the wings. With a little additional preparation, he can have them ready to go as the need arises.

But we're getting ahead of ourselves. Mr. Jaworsky is still planning. Now at step 4, he brainstorms as many ways as he can think of for students to demonstrate that they understand the principle of supply and demand. Mr. Jaworsky won't use all of these assessments; as with the list of potential instructional activities, he is building a library of potential assessment activities. In the end, he will have enough assessments to use some formatively and some for grading, and to use them flexibly according to student needs. Note, however, that all of these assessments are performances of understanding. Here is Mr. Jaworsky's initial list of ideas:

- State the principle of supply and demand in your words (orally or on a test).
- Identify an example of the principle of supply and demand (orally, on a test, or in an essay).
- Distinguish examples and nonexamples of the principle of supply and demand (orally, on a test, or in an essay).
- Predict an outcome based on the principle of supply and demand (on a test or as a performance assessment).
- Explain current events in terms of supply and demand (as a performance assessment).
- Write a scenario about a fictional country in the future in which events are driven by the principle of supply and demand (as a performance assessment).

Notice that none of the "differentiated" assessment methods is "dumbed down." In all of them, students demonstrate their level of understanding of supply and demand.

Some of the instructional activities from the list in step 3 could also be used for assessment if they included an appraisal method (for example, using rubrics).

The final step in Mr. Jaworsky's planning process is to decide how to evaluate students' final performance on the learning target. His school uses standards-based grading, so he customizes the school's general rubric for this learning target:

- **Advanced:** Shows a thorough understanding of the concept of supply and demand and extends understanding by relating supply and demand to other concepts, by offering new ideas, or by developing a deep and nuanced analysis.
- **Proficient:** Shows a complete and correct understanding of the concept of supply and demand. The student is poised for success on future standards and benchmarks in economics that build on this concept.
- **Nearing Proficiency:** Shows partial mastery of prerequisite knowledge (e.g., what goods and services are) and a rudimentary or incomplete understanding of the concept of supply and demand.
- **Novice:** Shows serious misconceptions about or a lack of understanding of the concept of supply and demand.

Like the library of instructional activities, this library of assessments is just a plan. As he did for the instructional activities, Mr. Jaworsky will make complete plans for each of the assessments that he decides to use, and he will leave the rest in the library. Each of the complete assessments he actually uses needs to be fit to the rubric: he must decide what level of performance on each test or performance assessment constitutes Advanced, Proficient, Nearing Proficiency, and Novice.

PUTTING IT ALL TOGETHER: A 5TH GRADE TEACHER DIFFERENTIATES INSTRUCTION

This example is based on an observation of a math lesson in Ms. North's self-contained 5th grade classroom. We have altered aspects of the lesson to make it a complete example of using a learning target to plan and implement differentiated instruction.

In accordance with the mathematics curriculum in her district, Ms. North is teaching about summarizing data. The objective listed in her lesson plan is "The student will use mean, median, and mode to describe a set of data." The "big idea" is that one statistic (a measure of central tendency) can summarize the "typical" value in a set of numbers, and which statistic to use depends on what kind of "typicality" is meant.

This concept has been introduced in prior grades (3rd and/or 4th) and is intended for mastery in grade 5.

IDENTIFY STUDENT NEEDS IN LIGHT OF THE LEARNING TARGET. Ms. North knows that three of her students will have trouble with calculations involving very large numbers; however, she believes that all of the students in her class are capable of understanding the concept of one summary number representing a set of numbers. She suspects that several of her students already mastered the concepts of mean, median, and mode when they were introduced in previous grades and are ready to extend this knowledge. She creates and administers a simple, five-item pre-test and finds that four students already know how to use mean, median, and mode.

PLAN INSTRUCTION WITH ATTENTION TO CONTENT, PROCESS, PRODUCT, AND LEARNING ENVIRONMENT. Here is the learning target that Ms. North derived from her instructional objective:

> I will be able to use a group of numbers to figure out
> - The mean, or the average;
> - The median, or the middle-most number; and
> - The mode, or the number you see the most of.

Ms. North writes three-tiered versions of a practice assignment (her performance of understanding), all a strong match with the intended learning outcome: using mean, median, and mode to describe a set of data. She plans a differentiated instructional sequence that follows a flow of instruction from whole class to small group and back again:

1. Whole class (10 minutes): Introduce the learning target, using the posting on the board. Pass back the pre-test, and work two of the problems together. Check for student understanding of the learning target by conducting a think-pair-share activity to generate definitions of mean, median, and mode; reasons for using them; and strategies for finding them.

2. Self-assessment (10 minutes): Students use a self-assessment sheet like the one in Figure 6.5.

6.5 Sample Student Self-Assessment Sheet

Name _____

My Self-Assessment

Try these problems, and then check what type of problem it was for you.

1. Find the mean, the median, and the mode for this set of numbers: 2, 10, 4, 2, 7.

Mean _____ Median _____ Mode _____

How is this problem for you?

☐   I can already do it easily.

☐   I can do it, and want more practice with this kind of problem.

☐   I can learn it, and want to practice this kind of problem with help.

☐   I am not ready for this kind of problem yet.

2. Jack sold newspapers at a newsstand. On Monday he sold 41 papers, on Tuesday he sold 58 papers, on Wednesday he sold 52 papers, on Thursday he sold 48 papers, on Friday he sold 57 papers, and on Saturday he sold 53 papers. On average, how many papers did he sell? _____ Is this number the mean, the median, or the mode? _____

How is this problem for you?

☐   I can already do it easily.

☐   I can do It, and want more practice with this kind of problem.

☐   I can learn it, and want to practice this kind of problem with help.

☐   I am not ready for this kind of problem yet.

3. Ms. Smith sold handmade jewelry at a shop. For the month of January, her sales totaled $163 the first week, $274 the second week, $873 the third week, and $842 the fourth week.

    a. Which statistic makes her sales look better, the mean or the median? _____ Explain how you figured this out.

    b. How many more dollars' worth of sales would Ms. Smith have to have made in January for her mean sales to equal $600? _____ Explain how you figured this out.

How is this problem for you?

☐   I can already do it easily.

☐   I can do it, and want more practice with this kind of problem.

☐   I can learn it, and want to practice this kind of problem with help.

☐   I am not ready for this kind of problem yet.

Ms. North's three-tiered versions of problem sets include problems similar to the ones in the self-assessment, not necessarily exact repeats of the same problem with slightly different numbers. In the self-assessment, students are assessing their general readiness, not "voting" on which problems they will do.

1. Small group (15–20 minutes): Based on their answers to the questions on the self-assessment, Ms. North places students into five groups: one group of students working on the first-level tiered practice set, with the teacher's help; two groups of students working on the midlevel tiered practice set, one with the teacher's help and one working on its own; and two groups of students working on the advanced-level tiered practice set, one with the teacher's help and one working on its own (this final group contains the four students identified by the pre-test as having mastered the concept).

2. Whole class (10 minutes): Students demonstrate their skill at using mean, median, and mode using a team game that has them working review questions at the board (questions prepared ahead of time, heterogeneous teams already assigned). Students have a chance to ask questions.

Ms. North's intention is that the following day, students will do independent work on tiered assignments, performances of understanding of mean, median, and mode at three levels. For some students, this work will be summative, demonstrating their proficiency and readiness to move on. Other students' performances may indicate that further practice is needed.

Ms. North teaches the lesson according to her plans for the day. She pays particular attention to communicating the learning target and, as criteria for success, tells students that they should be able to solve the problems in their problem sets and explain how they did it. She also uses the sample problems in the self-assessment as examples of the kinds of skills implied by the learning target. As she is circulating during the class, she talks with students about their own appraisals of the kinds of problems they are willing to tackle, providing special guidance to students who are tempted to undervalue or overvalue their skill levels.

EVALUATE THE LEARNING. The following day, each student independently completes the appropriate assignment. After students hand in their papers, Ms. North asks them to think together, in pairs and then in quads (two pairs), about what they found most useful in their quest to reach their learning target. Opinions vary, but most students are empowered by being able to choose their own learning level and say they would like to do it again.

In addition, Ms. North tells students that at the end of the unit, there will be a unit test that will include several central-tendency problems. She asks students to decide individually how they will preserve their new knowledge to be able to use it on the unit test at the end of next week. Students write their individual thoughts on exit tickets, which Ms. North will use to further differentiate review for the test.

LOOKING FORWARD

The learning target is the key for both teacher planning and student involvement in differentiated instruction. Aiming anywhere else, even in the name of student preference, will take the learning off track. Learning targets focus the teacher's thinking on how and when to differentiate, identify what the teacher asks students to focus on when differentiating a lesson, and focus the design of performances of understanding and criteria for success.

In Chapter 7, we explore how the processes of formative assessment and differentiated instruction work for learning targets that focus on higher-order thinking skills.

USING LEARNING TARGETS TO FOSTER HIGHER-ORDER THINKING

All learning targets should be judged according to how well they fit with curricular aims and how appropriate they are for students. However, it is particularly worth exploring learning targets about thinking skills. Historically, these have been difficult to teach and to assess (Brookhart, 2010b).

In this chapter, we explain how to establish and communicate learning targets that incorporate thinking skills in student-friendly terms and how to use formative assessment and differentiated instruction to help students reach thinking-skill targets. Specifically, we discuss

- How to establish, express, and communicate learning targets that are focused on thinking skills.
- How to articulate criteria for high-quality thinking.
- How higher-order thinking skills work across readiness levels (that is, how to avoid confusing "easy" and "hard" with level of cognition).
- How student self-assessment, goal setting, and other aspects of self-regulation require higher-order thinking.
- How to create substantive learning targets for creativity. (Brookhart, 2010b)

LEARNING TARGETS ABOUT THINKING SKILLS

Defining Higher-Order Thinking

Leighton (2011) points out that educational psychologists do not use the term *higher-order thinking*. Instead, they talk about the various cognitive processes underlying thinking. It is educators who have found the term useful because it helps teachers and students think about the kinds of things students will do with their knowledge.

Understanding higher-order thinking will help teachers incorporate thinking skills into their learning targets for students. Leighton reviewed the educational psychology literature to come up with a definition of higher-order thinking useful for assessment, with a question template for each aspect. Students use higher-order thinking when they

- Identify questions, assumptions, or issues to investigate. (They can ask, "What is to be verified, known, or investigated?")
- Systematically collect, analyze, and interpret evidence from a variety of perspectives. (They can ask, "Which are the best strategies for investigating claims to knowledge?")
- Develop coherent descriptions, inferences, predictions, explanations, evaluations, or arguments that are evidence-based, logical, and in context. (They can ask, "Which claims to knowledge does the evidence support?")
- Regulate and appreciate the cognitive effort required to substantiate claims to knowledge. (They can ask, "Is there value in seeking knowledge? Which strategies for investigating claims to knowledge enrich my process of knowing?")

Many other authors have also defined aspects of higher-order thinking, including Bransford and Stein (1984), Facione (2010), and Norris and Ennis (1989), to name just a few.

Establishing and Expressing Learning Targets About Thinking Skills

Before you can share learning targets about thinking skills with your students, you need to make sure that your instructional objectives incorporate thinking skills. The conventional way to incorporate thinking skills into instructional objectives is to use a taxonomy of thinking skills, such as Bloom's Revised Taxonomy (Anderson & Krathwohl, 2001) or Webb's Depth of Knowledge levels (Webb, 2002), often used for state test alignment studies. There are other taxonomies of thinking skills, too. What they all have in common is that they aim to help educators ensure that instruction and assessment go beyond memorization and recitation.

The hierarchical nature of these taxonomies has led to the terms *higher-order thinking* and—yuck!—*lower-order thinking*. We just hate the last term, because it implies that there is something "low" in value about knowing important facts, vocabulary, and concepts. There's nothing wrong with learning important facts.

What matters is making sure that learning doesn't stop there. Students should be able to use the facts and concepts they know to reason, figure things out, solve problems, write research questions and hypotheses, and so on. One of us (Brookhart, 2010b) has organized aspects of higher-order thinking this way:

- Functioning at the "top end" of a taxonomy of thinking skills (e.g., Bloom's Analysis, Evaluation, and Creation).
- Using logic and reasoning (e.g., induction and deduction).
- Using sound judgment (e.g., critical thinking).
- Identifying and solving problems.
- Being creative, seeing new patterns, and putting things together in a new way.

The following classroom example illustrates one way to go about designing a learning target that incorporates higher-order thinking.

Ms. Montoya is an 8th grade history teacher working on California curriculum content standard 8.10:

> Students analyze the multiple causes, key events, and complex consequences of the Civil War.

Item 4 under this strand reads,

> Discuss Abraham Lincoln's presidency and his significant writings and speeches and their relationship to the Declaration of Independence, such as his "House Divided" speech (1858), Gettysburg Address (1863), Emancipation Proclamation (1863), and inaugural addresses (1861 and 1865).

In addition to content standards, the California curriculum contains a critical thinking skills strand highlighting the importance of identifying and solving problems, judging information, and drawing conclusions.

Ms. Montoya plans a lesson on the Gettysburg Address (see Figure 7.1 for the text of the speech).

7.1 The Gettysburg Address

Abraham Lincoln gave this speech at the dedication of the Soldiers' National Cemetery in Gettysburg, Pennsylvania, on November 19, 1863. The Battle of Gettysburg was fought July 1–3, 1863. There were more casualties in the Battle of Gettysburg than in any other Civil War battle. Many historians see this battle as the turning point in the war, making a Union victory inevitable.

The Gettysburg Address has become famous for both the ideas Lincoln expressed and his eloquence in expressing them. This version of the text is the one on the walls of the Lincoln Memorial in Washington, D.C.

> Four score and seven years ago our fathers brought forth on this continent a new nation, conceived in liberty, and dedicated to the proposition that all men are created equal.
>
> Now we are engaged in a great civil war, testing whether that nation, or any nation so conceived and so dedicated, can long endure. We are met on a great battlefield of that war. We have come to dedicate a portion of that field as a final resting place for those who here gave their lives that that nation might live. It is altogether fitting and proper that we should do this.
>
> But, in a larger sense, we can not dedicate—we can not consecrate—we can not hallow—this ground. The brave men, living and dead, who struggled here, have consecrated it far above our poor power to add or detract. The world will little note nor long remember what we say here, but it can never forget what they did here. It is for us, the living, rather, to be dedicated here to the unfinished work which they who fought here have thus far so nobly advanced. It is rather for us to be here dedicated to the great task remaining before us—that from these honored dead we take increased devotion to that cause for which they gave the last full measure of devotion—that we here highly resolve that these dead shall not have died in vain— that this nation, under God, shall have a new birth of freedom—and that government of the people, by the people, for the people, shall not perish from the earth.

Even confining her lesson to the Gettysburg Address, there are a lot of potential learning targets in content standard 8.10.4. Ms. Montoya decides she wants all students to understand the literal text of the Gettysburg Address and to engage in higher-order thinking about it. Here are her learning intentions for all students, per her curriculum:

Curriculum goal: Discuss Abraham Lincoln's presidency and his significant writings and speeches and their relationship to the Declaration of Independence, such as his "House Divided" speech (1858), Gettysburg Address (1863), Emancipation Proclamation (1863), and inaugural addresses (1861 and 1865).

Instructional objectives for the lesson: The student will be able to

- Explain the literal meaning of the text of the Gettysburg Address. [Comprehension level]
- Make connections among ideas in the Gettysburg Address and other historical and/or contemporary ideas (e.g., in the Declaration of Independence or other documents and/or in current events). [Higher-order thinking]

Using the brainstorming planning method described in Chapter 6, Ms. Montoya comes up with instructional objectives, a library of potential instructional activities, and a library of potential assessment activities. At this point, she is establishing her instructional intentions with the potential to differentiate across a range of student backgrounds, interests, and readiness levels. Figure 7.2 shows the results of her brainstorming.

Now it's time for Ms. Montoya to select the instructional activities and assessments she will use. To differentiate, she uses a method like Ms. North's in Chapter 6. She will require all students to complete Activity 1, which she will assess with oral questioning, and one of the versions (or tiers) of Activity 2, which she will assess with rubrics. She will ask students to assess their interest in working on Activities 3, 4, and 5 and then, as much as possible, assign each student to a project according to his or her choice. At this point, she needs to complete directions, success criteria, and rubrics for each activity, making sure to build formative assessment opportunities into the directions.

Communicating Learning Targets About Thinking Skills

As the last step in her planning, Ms. Montoya must turn her teacher-facing instructional objectives into student-facing learning targets. She might set the context by

7.2 List of Potential Instructional Activities and Assessments for Gettysburg Address Lesson

Teacher's Instructional Objectives

    a. Explain the literal meaning of the text of the Gettysburg Address. [Comprehension level]

    b. Make connections among ideas in the Gettysburg Address and other historical and/or contemporary ideas (e.g., in the Declaration of Independence or other documents and/or in current events). [Higher-order thinking]

Potential Instructional Activities

1. Group "unpacking" of text. Sentence by sentence, students in pairs or small groups put the text into their own words. They either look up or figure out the meaning of unfamiliar vocabulary. [Oral or written activity, obj. a.]

2. Give students the text of the Declaration of Independence. Ask them to identify as many points as they can in the Gettysburg Address that refer to something in the Declaration of Independence, and show and explain the connections. Possible adaptation: ask students with below-grade reading skills to concentrate on the first sentence in the Gettysburg Address and the preamble to the Declaration. [Written project, obj. a, b.]

3. Pretend you are making a bulletin board for a class that is studying the Gettysburg Address. In the style of a graphic novel, draw panels that illustrate the speech. Be prepared to explain your drawings. [Representational project and oral presentation, obj. a. Note: This project is even better if students create a real bulletin board.]

4. What effect does the message of the Gettysburg Address have on you, reading it today? Can you find any quotes from more recent presidents expressing similar ideas about soldiers who gave their lives in wars? What do you think are the effects of these comments on family members of the soldiers and on U.S. citizens in general? [Written project or oral presentation, obj. a, b.]

5. Lincoln's phrase "government of the people, by the people, for the people" became a very famous expression about democracy. (1) Using the Internet and the library, find out what sources historians think influenced him to use that phrase. Describe these sources and how they relate to Lincoln and his speech. (2) Although this phrase is not in the Declaration of Independence, show how the phrase also echoes some of the ideas in the Declaration. (3) Given what you know about Lincoln's political views, why do you think he decided to end his speech with this powerful rhetorical device? [Extended written project or paper, obj. a, b.]

Potential Assessments

1. Conduct in-class oral questioning, preparing questions ahead of time.

2. Build performance assessment opportunities into instructional activities 2, 3, 4, or 5 (above).

    a. Use criteria to construct rubrics for giving feedback during work.

    b. Use the same rubrics to score or grade the final product.

3. Use selected- or constructed-response questions on the unit test.

reminding students of other speeches and other aspects of Lincoln's presidency that they have studied.

Because the instructional objectives describe complex processes, it is not enough just to preface them with "I can" (e.g., "I can explain the literal meaning of the text of the Gettysburg Address"). Ms. Montoya needs to show students what the objectives mean for them. Here is one example of how the instructional objectives for the lesson might be rewritten as a general learning target for students. Aspects of this target would be adapted for each day's lesson, and the daily learning targets would match the performances of understanding for each lesson.

> My learning target is to understand what the Gettysburg Address meant in 1863 and what it means today. I will know I have hit the target when
>
> ☑ I can put the speech into my own words.
> ☑ I can explain how the Gettysburg Address echoes some ideas from the Declaration of Independence and other historical documents.
> ☑ I can explain why the Gettysburg Address still affects people today.

All the potential activities and assessments that Ms. Montoya has planned serve this learning target. Not all students will learn exactly the same content details and processing skills (e.g., writing, speaking, and representing), but at the end of the lesson, they should all be able to say "I can" do those three things. If not, they should be able to say, "I cannot do this yet, so here's what I need to do now."

ARTICULATING CRITERIA FOR HIGH-QUALITY THINKING

The three success criteria in Ms. Montoya's learning target for the Gettysburg Address lesson are based on her instructional objectives. The instructional activities all serve these criteria, but they differ in their specific emphases and in the processes and products they require. Ms. Montoya will use Activities 2, 3, 4, and 5 with criteria and rubrics, with clear performance levels and some mechanism (e.g., self-reflection) for students to analyze the relationship between their work on these activities and their learning targets.

For the sake of space, we will work out rubrics for just Activity 2; the processes for the other activities would be similar. Activity 2 has students mostly working on the meaning of the Gettysburg Address and its relation to the Declaration of Independence. Connections to today are indirect (we still live in a society that espouses the Declaration and values a democratic government) and are not explicitly part of this assignment.

Criteria for good work include identifying aspects of the Gettysburg Address that echo the language and/or ideas of the Declaration, identifying those particular parts of the Declaration, and clearly explaining the connections. One approach to creating a rubric would be simply to add performance-level descriptions to the criteria (see Figure 7.3).

7.3 Sample Rubric: Performance-Level Descriptions Added to Success Criteria

	2	1	0
Evidence from the Gettysburg Address	All (or most) relevant points are selected from the Gettysburg Address and correctly interpreted.	Some relevant points are selected from the Gettysburg Address and correctly interpreted.	Few (or no) relevant points are selected from the Gettysburg Address and/or points are not correctly interpreted.
Evidence from the Declaration of Independence	All (or most) relevant points are selected from the Declaration.	Some relevant points are selected from the Declaration.	Few (or no) relevant points are selected from the Declaration.
Logic and clarity of explanation	The way in which the points are connected is clear, logical, and well explained.	The way in which the points are connected is mostly clear and logical. Some explanation is given.	The way in which the points are connected is unclear, illogical, and/or not explained.

The rubric could incorporate one or two more performance levels, depending on grading and reporting needs. These rubrics are general, meaning that they can and should be shared with students at the time the project is assigned. They provide more detail about the criteria for success on one learning target: "I can explain how the Gettysburg Address echoes some ideas from the Declaration of Independence."

As an aside, it is possible for rubrics to be task-specific rather than general. For example, task-specific rubrics might read

> Notes that "conceived in liberty, and dedicated to the proposition that all men are created equal" echoes the first sentence of the preamble to the Declaration ("We hold these truths to be self-evident, that all men are created equal, that they are endowed by their Creator with certain unalienable Rights, that among these are Life, Liberty and the pursuit of Happiness").

We do not recommend writing task-specific rubrics, however. Students should be aiming for the general thinking skill of identifying all relevant evidence. Task-specific rubrics reduce thinking to meeting a checklist of "right" answers, removing judgment and critical thinking from the task. In some ways, they might seem easier to write, but because they are merely grading criteria for teachers and cannot be shared with students, they cannot function as criteria for success, and students miss out on important learning benefits.

UNDERSTANDING HIGHER-ORDER THINKING ACROSS READINESS LEVELS

The most important aspect of this Gettysburg Address lesson is that it shows that students at *all* readiness levels should aim for learning targets involving higher-order thinking skills. Students who, for example, struggle with reading should not spend all their time trying to comprehend the text and miss the main point of studying it in the first place. The Gettysburg Address is famous partly for its rhetoric, but its place in the curriculum is due mainly to its significance in advancing the argument for democracy, begun in the Declaration of Independence, at a time when the success of the United States' experiment with democracy was in question. Without getting the opportunity to engage with that point, why should a struggling reader struggle to read the speech at all?

Many people have a misconception that "higher-order" thinking is necessarily more difficult than recall. Another common misconception is that students have to first "learn" (i.e., recall) facts and concepts before they can learn to apply them. Neither of these ideas is true. Level of difficulty and level of thinking are two different aspects of learning targets. The best learning involves students in acquiring and using facts simultaneously. Applying new knowledge helps students see the purpose of learning it in the first place.

Educators who hold either of these misconceptions risk shortchanging young students and low achievers of any age. Students who must slog through recall and drill assignments before they are deemed "ready" to do higher-order thinking will learn that school is boring. And they will not learn to think well.

Figure 7.4 (p. 124) gives several examples of easier and more difficult questions and tasks for the Gettysburg Address example we have been looking at. These are questions that could be asked orally (assessment method 1 in Figure 7.2). Ms. Montoya prepares questions ahead of time as part of her lesson planning. Writing good questions that are directly related to the learning targets takes thought. If you wait until you are in front of a class, your questions won't always hit the target. Notice that each of the questions in Figure 7.4—whether easier or more difficult, recall or thinking—goes directly to either students' understanding of the meaning of the text or students' understanding of the text's connection to the larger argument for democracy. In short, each of the questions helps both students and teacher gather information about how students are progressing toward the learning targets.

Figure 7.4 also includes some examples of questions that engage students at different levels of depth and complexity, allowing multiple "ways in" for students with various backgrounds and readiness levels. These examples show that teachers should ask *all* students questions that require thought, not merely recall.

HIGHER-ORDER THINKING AND THE LEARNING PROCESS

Higher-order thinking enables students to regulate their own learning processes. Metacognition, or "thinking about thinking," requires reasoning about abstract concepts (like considering, "How well am I understanding this part?"), which is necessary for student self-assessment. Goal setting and other aspects of self-regulation require higher-order thinking, specifically the acts of coming up with and then carrying out a plan that the student can reasonably expect to lead to improvement. In a real sense, "how to learn" becomes a learning target in its own right.

The higher-order thinking skills involved in self-regulated learning can be organized in several ways. Boekaerts's (1999) model is used in much self-regulation research and also has clear implications for classroom instruction and assessment. She describes three types of strategies that self-regulated learners need:

7.4 Examples of Recall and Higher-Order Thinking Questions for the Gettysburg Address Lesson

	Easy	Difficult	Answerable on Multiple Levels
Recall	Lincoln says, "We are met on a great battlefield." What was the name of the battlefield, and why were they meeting there? Lincoln says, "The world will little note nor long remember what we say here." Did that turn out to be true? How do you know?	"Four score and seven years ago" is an archaic way to indicate a number. What number is "four score and seven"? In what other place in literature would you find a number expressed in this way?	Can you tell me an unfamiliar word or a phrase that isn't clear to you in this speech? Lincoln talks about "the great task remaining before us." What did he say this task was?
Higher-Order Thinking	Lincoln's speech was given at the dedication of a cemetery. But his main point ended up being about a free and democratic government. How did he make the connection between fallen soldiers and the government? Do you think he made this connection clearly in his speech? Why do you think Lincoln took the opportunity of giving this speech to talk about a free and democratic government?	Lincoln uses imagery of the human life cycle (birth, life, death) to describe the nation. Find and explain as many examples of these images as you can. Why do you think he uses these life-cycle images for the nation in this particular speech?	How are you going to find out the meaning of the unfamiliar word or phrase you've chosen? Why do you think the United States and other countries honor their soldiers who died in battle?

- First, self-regulated learners need *cognitive* strategies. Students use cognitive strategies to deal directly with the knowledge and skills they are learning. Cognitive strategies include rehearsal (copying, underlining, and repeating facts); elaboration (paraphrasing and summarizing material); and organiza-tion (outlining and problem solving).

- Second, self-regulated learners need *metacognitive* strategies. Metacognitive strategies include planning (deciding what to do and in what order and with what resources); monitoring comprehension and performance; and evaluat-ing the quality of one's learning.
- Third, self-regulated learners need *motivational* strategies. Students need to have the expectation that they can learn the content or perform the skill to be attained. They need to value the learning, seeing the knowledge or skill as important, either in its own right or for its instrumental value in getting to some other goal—as, for example, a student who wants to be an engineer knows that it is important to learn calculus. Students need to have positive affective responses to the learning—interest, enjoyment, or some other posi-tive emotion.

Dignath and Büttner (2008) conducted a meta-analysis of studies of the effects of training in self-regulation on students' academic performance, strategy use, and motivation. They analyzed 49 studies of primary school students and 35 studies of secondary school students, in all involving more than 8,600 students. They found, overall, that self-regulation training did affect all these outcomes. The average effect size was 0.69, or the equivalent of moving from the 50th percentile to the 75th percen-tile on a standardized measure. They also found some interesting differences in results between primary and secondary school students. Two of these seem particularly relevant to our discussion of learning targets.

First, for primary school students, effects were stronger if strategy training was part of the treatment, whereas for secondary school students, effects were stronger if reflection training was part of the treatment. Dignath and Büttner (2008) reasoned that younger students were still broadening their repertoires of self-regulation strategies, whereas older students already had strategy repertoires and needed to learn how to use their strategies more effectively.

Second, for primary school students, effects of self-regulation training were stronger in math than in reading, whereas for secondary school students, effects of self-regulation training were stronger in reading than in math. Dignath and Büttner (2008) reasoned that younger students acquired math learning strategies while they learned math, whereas older students started applying text-comprehension strategies only after they had already learned basic reading skills. Some readers may be familiar with teaching young children "reading strategies" and wonder about this finding. To be clear, the strategies investigated in this meta-analysis were cognitive, metacognitive, and motivational strategies for the self-regulation of learning, not reading strategies like finger-tracking or sounding out words.

Our purpose here is not to present a complete review of the self-regulation literature. Rather, the important point is that these studies demonstrate that self-regulation skills are teachable and learnable. That means they can and should be learning targets! Most teachers want to teach cognitive awareness and metacognition and develop their students' motivation for learning, but they don't usually use this self-regulation vocabulary with students. Instead, teachers call these skills "work habits."

As with any teachable and learnable knowledge or skill, metacognitive and self-regulatory strategies should be presented as learning targets that students can aim for with attainable criteria for success. Figure 7.5 lists just a few examples of the many ways to express work habits as learning targets and criteria for success.

One of us once conducted a workshop with teachers who were just beginning to use a standards-based grading system. The teachers were to use grades in the form of proficiency levels (Beginning, Basic, Proficient, and Advanced) to report achievement of the standards. A Learning Skills Assessment was also included, which effectively made learning targets out of a list of skills related to effort, process, problem solving, and responsibility. We engaged in an exercise in which groups of teachers tried to come up with criteria for success for the learning skills listed, although we didn't use the term *criteria for success*. We just discussed evidence of the skills: "What would you look for to rate a student on this skill?"

The teachers found it difficult to list evidence ("look-fors") for most of the learning skills. Without criteria for success, work habits cannot be effective learning targets. For example, one of the skills on the list was "takes responsibility for own actions." Without criteria, if a student scored a 3 ("frequently") instead of a 4 ("most of the time") on this indicator and asked, "How could I get better?", all the teacher could do would be to restate the learning target—something like, "Take more responsibility for your own actions."

By the end of the exercise, the teachers began to realize that they needed criteria for success—things to look for and to communicate to students. They also began to realize that they did have ideas about what these were, but they were not used to articulating them for students.

7.5 Sample Learning Targets and Criteria for Success for Some Self-Regulation Skills

Self-Regulation Skill	Sample Learning Targets	Sample Criteria for Success
Cognitive strategies: • Rehearsal • Elaboration • Organization	I can take notes effectively.	• My notes are clear and readable. • My notes are detailed enough to study from. • My notes highlight important points or concepts. • My notes are organized into topic areas [or chronologically, or whatever is appropriate].
	I can study effectively.	• I read my notes and quiz myself until I'm sure I understand the material. • I give the right amount of time and energy to studying. • When I study, I do better on tests than when I don't.
Metacognitive strategies: • Planning • Self-monitoring • Self-evaluation	I can set goals and work toward them.	• Before I start work on an assignment, I stop and figure out what I'm supposed to be doing. • I can chunk work into manageable pieces. • I set time lines and follow them. • I complete work on time.
	I can keep track of my own learning progress.	• I look at feedback and grades on previous work and compare them with my own idea of how I did. • I use my performance on previous work to decide how to use my time and effort on new work. • I keep a chart or graph of my grades and use it to help me plan my work. • I feel responsible for the quality of my own work.

continued

7.5 Sample Learning Targets and Criteria for Success for Some Self-Regulation Skills (*continued*)

Self-Regulation Skill	Sample Learning Targets	Sample Criteria for Success
Motivational strategies: • Defining expectations • Establishing value • Ascertaining interest	I can figure out why it's important to learn the things I study in school.	• I look for connections between new topics of study and things I already know. • I figure out why it's important to learn new material, and if I can't figure it out, I ask my teacher.
	I can use my interests to help me in school.	• I know what topics I am interested in. • I keep an open mind about new topics I study and try to develop new interests.

We share this story as a cautionary tale. Students need learning targets and criteria for success for learning skills and work habits. It may be unusual in your school, as it was in this school, to think in those terms, and it may take more time and thought than you imagine (everybody knows what good work habits are, don't they?). But treating learning-how-to-learn skills as learning targets with their own criteria for success can be done, and your students will reap the benefits.

CREATIVITY IN LEARNING TARGETS

Before we illustrate how to design learning targets for creativity, let's look at an example of something that is *not* a creativity learning target.

A secondary English teacher introduces a unit on poetry by asking her students to work in groups to make posters depicting Edgar Allan Poe's life. She gives the students a rubric that includes both "content" and "creativity" criteria. The content criterion is about having accurate information on the poster, and the creativity criterion is about the poster being colorful, engaging, and visually appealing.

We can't tell you how many times we have seen examples of "creativity" rubrics and criteria that were about being artistic or visually appealing. Putting a picture on a report cover, using good design skills for making posters, incorporating bright colors into a display—these are all great things, but they're not criteria for the learning target of working creatively. They are criteria for visual design and display skills. Similarly, we have seen rubrics for written work with "creativity" as one of the criteria, used to mean that the writing was interesting or persuasive. Writing in an interesting or persuasive manner is great—but again, it is not creativity.

Creativity is about defining problems or tasks in a new light and putting ideas together in new ways. Creativity is *not* being cute, artistic, or even interesting. The misconception that creativity means making things appealing—whether visually, as in a beautiful report cover, or verbally, as in a tug-at-the-heartstrings story—often leads to the assignment of "points" for creativity in work that is not, in fact, creative.

Students who are creative

- Recognize the importance of a deep knowledge base and continually work to learn new things.
- Are open to new ideas and actively seek them out.
- Find source material for ideas in a wide variety of media, people, and events.
- Look for ways to organize and reorganize ideas into different categories and combinations, and then evaluate whether the results are interesting, new, or helpful.
- Use trial and error when they are not sure of how to proceed, viewing failure as an opportunity to learn. (Brookhart, 2010b)

Aspects of these skills can become learning targets. Students can learn to look for what is "new" about the work of authors, artists, scientists, historians, and mathematicians. They can learn to try for "new" applications or cross-references in their own work. We shortchange students when we communicate in our words and in our assignments that creativity means visual or verbal pizzazz. True creativity is what moves society forward, and students will not develop their creativity unless they aim for it like any other learning target.

If you want students to be creative, assign work that requires them to produce a new product or reorganize existing ideas (not just facts on a poster or bulletin board) in a new way. Make creativity an explicit learning target. Allow or even require students to find and use source material beyond a set of assigned readings. Above all, make sure that the generation of new ideas—whether in writing, speech, illustration, or construction—connects to the rest of the content that the student is supposed to be learning and not to something tangential like the cover or the format of a project.

As an example, let's return to the lesson on Edgar Allan Poe's poem "The Bells" that we discussed in Chapter 2. Recall that the teacher said,

> Today, our learning target is to be able to describe how Poe thought and felt about different kinds of bells, and to explain how we can figure that out from his poem. We'll know we are successful when we can explain how imagery from the poem creates thoughts and feelings for readers in as much detail as we just explained how real bells conjure up thoughts and feelings in us.

Let's assume that the students have just experienced a wonderful lesson and can explain how imagery in the poem evokes thoughts and feelings in readers. They are ready for another learning target in this unit on poetry and imagery. They are ready to create their own poems.

The teacher says, "Think of a sound that is common in your life, in the same way that the sounds of bells were common in Edgar Allan Poe's life." Juxtaposing Poe's context and the students' lives will be fertile ground for creative work. Then she says, "Select at least two of the poetic devices in 'The Bells' and use them in a poem describing your sound." This part of the assignment reflects the content. Students will need to use some combination of alliteration, assonance, onomatopoeia, metaphor, or any of the other poetic devices they studied in an appropriate way.

The teacher needs to flesh out complete directions for the assignment, of course. For our purposes, we are mostly concerned with the learning target and the criteria for success expressing to students, in terms they can understand, what creative work should look like. Here are a possible learning target and success criteria for this lesson:

I can write poetry that shows other people what I think and feel when I hear [student-selected sound]. I will know I have done this well when

- ☑ My poem uses [student-selected poetic devices] similarly to the way Poe's did. (Content criterion)
- ☑ My [student-selected poetic devices] appeal to my readers' senses. (Content criterion)
- ☑ My poem is not like anyone else's and reflects a special sound in my life. (Creativity criterion)
- ☑ My poem surprises readers in some way. (Creativity criterion)

To further communicate the learning target and criteria for success, the teacher might draft two or three examples of varying quality and have students discuss how the examples meet or don't meet the criteria.

LOOKING FORWARD

In this chapter and the previous one, we have shown that every step of instruction and formative assessment should be grounded in a learning target. But at some point, instruction must end. At the end of the instruction, it's time for summative assessment—time to ascertain and report what students have learned. In most classrooms and schools, that means grading, which is the subject of Chapter 8.

8

USING LEARNING TARGETS TO GUIDE SUMMATIVE ASSESSMENT AND GRADING

It's only fair to base students' grades on the same learning targets that they have aimed for. It makes no sense to have students try to learn one thing and then grade them on another.

Achievement categories on report cards are broader than single-lesson learning targets, whether those categories are traditional subject designations (e.g., mathematics) or more specific reporting standards (e.g., problem solving). Therefore, to truly base classroom summative assessment and grading on the learning targets students actually worked toward, you need to do two things. First, design classroom summative assessments to summarize achievement over a set of learning targets. Second, aggregate the grades from those summative assessments using a method that will result in a final report card grade that keeps the learning targets in balance.

WHAT SHOULD GRADES MEAN?

Grades are supposed to communicate student achievement of state standards and curricular learning goals (not to be confused with the narrower student learning targets) (Brookhart, 2011; O'Connor, 2009). Often, grades don't reflect learning. Many teachers add points or credits that reflect effort and behavior (Brookhart, 2009) so that the meaning of the resulting grade is not clear. Report cards need not report only academic learning outcomes, but effort and behavior and progress or improvement should be reported in separate sections, using different symbols from the academic grades, if desired.

Learning targets help clarify the grading process. Taking learning targets seriously leads to a grading philosophy rooted in the following beliefs:

- Academic grades should be based on achievement of learning goals.
- Effort and behavior should be assessed separately and handled by working with the student.

In the next section, we lay out the connections between using learning targets in the classroom and grading on achievement. A full treatment of why grades should reflect achievement is beyond the scope of this chapter, but if you are interested in reading more on the subject, see Chapters 1–3 in Brookhart (2011).

LEARNING TARGETS AND GRADES

Learning targets are the connection between daily learning and the reportable achievement of learning goals. Today's learning target should build on yesterday's learning target, and any one learning target should fit into a learning trajectory that goes on to something bigger—at some point, something big enough to be reported. Having a learning target that is part of such a trajectory is part of a lesson's "reason to live."

For example, let's say a district uses a standards-based report card with two science standards: Concepts and Processes and Science as Inquiry. During this report period, a 3rd grade class has been studying energy concepts and processes, including the different forms of energy, how they can be described, and how energy can be transferred from one place to another or transformed from one form to another. Students have been learning to identify and describe these energy forms and processes in everyday life—for example, the way a lightbulb uses electricity and gives off light and heat. Each of these learning standards has been supported by a series of lessons, each with its own learning target.

At the same time, students have been learning science inquiry skills like formulating questions, making predictions, collecting and interpreting data, using evidence to create and evaluate scientific explanations, and making models and representations. They have used these process skills during the same lessons in which they have worked on their understanding of energy.

The students' report card grades for science should reflect their developing understanding of both energy and science inquiry. From the students' point of view, the rationale is simple:

- You (the teacher) asked me to learn these things.
- How well did I do?

From the teacher's point of view, the main points are the same. Below, we list the line of reasoning that leads from learning targets to achievement-focused grading practices.

- I (the teacher) asked you to learn these things.
  — I shared learning targets with you, in a sequence that makes sense.
  — I presented you with learning opportunities and used strong performances of understanding.
  — I gave you feedback on your work based on the learning targets.
  — I gave you opportunities for self-assessment based on the learning targets.
- After all this, I will assign a grade that summarizes how well you learned.
  — I will design summative assessments that check on your level of attainment of the learning targets, individually or in clusters that make sense.
  — I will put the grades for these summative assessments together in such a way that the summary grade is the best indicator of your achievement level that is possible with the symbol system we use in our school.
  — I will communicate additional information (because one summary grade can't tell everything) in comments and in conferences with you and your parents, as needed.

Up to this point in the book, we have emphasized the reasoning delineated in the first two bullets. We have described learning targets and performances of understanding and explained how they are the means by which teachers design learning tasks for students, students engage in the learning tasks, and students make sense out of their learning.

But the intent of these learning targets would be nullified if we didn't also honor them in summative assessment and grading. In the following sections, we provide guidance on how to design summative assessments that yield grades that are faithful to your students' learning targets and how to aggregate those grades into a reportable summary that is, in turn, faithful to those learning targets.

SUMMATIVE ASSESSMENTS: THE "INGREDIENTS" FOR GRADES

Designing summative assessments that summarize achievement over a set of learning targets involves two general principles:

1. For each summative assessment, use a plan, or blueprint, that faithfully represents the learning goals toward which the lesson-level learning targets were aimed.

2. Write test items or performance tasks that elicit the intended performances, and create scoring rubrics that give credit to all intended aspects of the performances.

Planning Summative Assessments That Represent the Learning Goals

In your instructional planning, you derive unit goals from state standards and curriculum goals. Then you derive teacher instructional objectives and student learning targets from those unit goals. You make sure that students are engaging in strong performances of understanding that focus their work on the learning target and at the same time yield evidence of student progress toward the learning target.

For summative assessment, you reassemble what has been pulled apart for instruction and formative assessment at a higher level. Summative assessments that faithfully represent learning goals are analogous to performances of understanding that faithfully represent learning targets. The unit is larger than the lesson, encompassing understanding of a set of learning targets or a more complex learning goal farther along the learning trajectory. But the principle is the same.

Recall Figure 2.1 (p. 29), which illustrates how each day's lesson feeds learning forward toward increasingly more complex understanding and skills. Like most formative assessment, most daily performances of understanding focus on small pieces of knowledge or aspects of skills. The reason for this narrower focus is that the main purpose of performances of understanding is learning—not grading—and understanding these small chunks of knowledge is necessary to support next steps in learning. In contrast, summative assessment typically addresses larger chunks of knowledge or more integrated skills, because the purpose of summative assessment is to ascertain what has been learned. You could call summative assessments "meta-performances of understanding."

To assemble the chunks students have learned into a valid indicator of integrated knowledge and skill, you need a plan—typically called an *assessment blueprint*. Assessment blueprints are useful for planning both tests and performance assessments. There are many ways to draw up an assessment blueprint. We explain two of them here, focusing especially on the way they enable you to plan how the learning targets come together into a larger indicator that is both representative of the learning students did and meaningful on its own as a summary measure.

Figure 8.1 presents a template for a two-dimensional blueprint organized by both the content and the thinking skills to be assessed. This is the model we recommend, because it forces you to think about both content and thinking skills. Figure 8.2 (p. 138) presents a template for a one-dimensional blueprint. These take less time to use and are appropriate for designing some simple assessments, especially assessments of recall of facts and concepts. The downside is that the structure in Figure 8.2 does not force explicit consideration of thinking skills.

As you can see, either blueprint allows you to allocate learning targets to standards and to sort points by standard. The two-dimensional blueprint also lets you sort points by cognitive level. You can easily see which percentage of the total score on the assessment corresponds with which learning target and cognitive level, and adjust the balance *before* you write the test questions or performance tasks. This is the beauty of a blueprint! Once you have the balance right, you can write test questions or performance tasks "to order," according to the specifications laid out in the blueprint.

The use of percentages in blueprints does *not* mean that the assessment needs to be scored on the percent scale. The blueprint points and percentages describe the balance of credit given in the assessment's score, no matter what method of scoring is used. What the blueprint describes is *percentage of the assessment*—that is, which percentage of a summative assessment's grade is based on which learning targets and standards. Unfortunately, using percentages for planning in blueprints can be a source of confusion for people who are used to thinking of all grades as percentages. We don't encourage this line of thinking!

8.1 Template for a Two-Dimensional Assessment Blueprint for One Summative Assessment

Content Outline	Cognitive Level				Total Points	%
	[Use Bloom, Webb, or any other appropricte classification scheme. Only use cells where learning targets fit. Not all cells will be filled.]					
	Knowledge	Comprehension	Application	Analysis		
Specific knowledge or skill standard assessed	Learning target(s) that addressed recall of facts and concepts for this standard [Number of points for this portion of the assessment's score]	Learning target(s) that addressed comprehension for this standard [Number of points for this portion of the assessment's score]	Learning target(s) that addressed application for this standard [Number of points for this portion of the assessment's score]	Learning target(s) that addressed analysis for this standard [Number of points for this portion of the assessment's score]	Sum of row points	Percentage of total points
Specific knowledge or skill standard assessed	Learning target(s) [Number of points]	Learning target(s) [Number of points]	Learning target(s) [Number of points]	Learning target(s) [Number of points]	Sum of row points	Percentage of total points
[Use as many rows as necessary for the assessment]	Learning target(s) [Number of points]	Learning target(s) [Number of points]	Learning target(s) [Number of points]	Learning target(s) [Number of points]	Sum of row points	Percentage of total points
Total Points	Sum of column points	Sum of column points	Sum of column points	Sum of column points	Total points	100%
%	Percentage of total points	Percentage of total points	Percentage of total points	Percentage of total points		

8.2 Template for a One-Dimensional Assessment Blueprint

Outline	Total Points	%
Specific knowledge or skill standard assessed • Learning target for this standard [Number of points for this portion of the assessment's score] • Learning target for this standard [Number of points for this portion of the assessment's score] • Learning target for this standard [Number of points for this portion of the assessment's score] • [List as many learning targets as necessary.]	**Sum of points for this standard**	**Percentage of total points**
Specific knowledge or skill standard assessed • Learning target for this standard [Number of points for this portion of the assessment's score] • Learning target for this standard [Number of points for this portion of the assessment's score] • Learning target for this standard [Number of points for this portion of the assessment's score] • [List as many learning targets as necessary.]	**Sum of points for this standard**	**Percentage of total points**
[Use as many rows as necessary for the assessment.]	**Sum of points for this standard**	**Percentage of total points**
Total	**Total points**	**100**

Writing Test Items and Performance Tasks That Match Intended Assessment Outcomes

The blueprint is a great first step. Your second step is to faithfully represent the specifications in your plan in well-crafted questions and performance tasks. These questions and tasks apply the "performance of understanding" principle writ large.

The following examples illustrate how high-quality blueprints enable you to plan assessments that link to standards and the learning targets you used to teach those standards.

EXAMPLE OF A TEST BLUEPRINT. Figure 8.3 (p. 140) shows a blueprint constructed for a 5th grade unit on weather. Note that it relates the learning targets that were taught in the unit to standards (in this example, the California 5th grade earth science standards).

This blueprint contains major decisions about the unit test you will write. It allows you to allocate the relative emphases you want the various learning targets to have in the test score, using the points and percentage columns at the right of the blueprint. (Note that the percentages in this example sum to 99%, not 100%, just because of rounding error.) If the proportions don't look right, you can change them while you are still at the blueprint stage, before you have taken the time to write or find good test questions. In this example, there is slightly more emphasis on clouds and different types of precipitation than on basic facts about the atmosphere, which represents the way the unit was taught.

A test blueprint also allows you to allocate the proportions of the test that will tap various kinds of thinking or cognitive processing, using the points and percentage rows at the bottom of the blueprint. In this example, we used the first four levels of Bloom's taxonomy, with slightly more emphasis on comprehension and slightly less emphasis on analysis. We didn't use the other two levels (evaluation and creation), because there will be no questions on the test at those levels. However, the weather unit could include a project that would assess original creation (perhaps of an original weather map and related scenarios and predictions) in addition to the test. For most units, the unit test would not be the only summative assessment.

Note that not all of the blueprint's cells are filled. That's because the goal is not to fill cells but to appropriately organize the learning targets for the unit so that you know what you are assessing and can write questions accordingly.

Writing the questions is the next step. For each of the filled-in cells, write or select questions that are mini–performances of understanding for the content and cognitive

8.3 Example of a Test Blueprint for a 5th Grade Unit Test on Weather

Content Outline	Cognitive Level				Total Points	%
	Knowledge	Comprehension	Application	Analysis		
Atmosphere [Ref: CA earth science standard 5.4]	Identifies definitions for vocabulary and key terms. [2 points]	Describes how the sun warms the earth's surface. [3 points]	Solves scenario-based problems about why one place gets hotter than another. [2 points]		7 points	21%
Air pressure and wind [Ref: CA earth science standard 5.4]	Identifies definitions for vocabulary and key terms. [2 points]	Identifies what causes wind direction and speed. [3 points]	Interprets weather station models and interprets isobars on a weather map. [3 points]		8 points	24%
Water vapor and humidity [Ref: CA earth science standard 5.3]	Identifies definitions for vocabulary and key terms. [2 points]	Identifies where water vapor in the air comes from and explains different ways in which water vapor changes form. [3 points]	Solves problems involving relative humidity. [3 points]		8 points	24%
Clouds and precipitation [Ref: CA earth science standards 5.3 and 5.4]	Identifies definitions for vocabulary and key terms. [2 points]	Explains how different conditions produce different forms of precipitation. [3 points]		Analyzes real-world weather conditions according to the processes in the water cycle. [5 points]	10 points	30%
Total Points	8 points	12 points	8 points	5 points	33 points	100%
%	24%	36%	24%	15%		

level specified. You will see that sampling is built into this blueprint. There are 8 total points for vocabulary and key terms, 2 points for four topics. In all, in this unit there were 25 new vocabulary terms, but putting them all on the test would leave room for little else. If students know that vocabulary and key terms will be on the test, but not which ones, they will study all 25 and be prepared for the 8 that are sampled. This, by the way, is the reason why tests are usually secured. It's not because of any need for stealth or conspiracy. It is simply that if students knew which eight words would be tested, they would study only those (in fact, it would be silly for them not to), and those 8 points would no longer be a proxy for testing the whole domain.

When you write questions for each of the cells, understand that the purpose of the point allocation is to have the overall test score reflect the desired emphases. This does not mean that there needs to be as many questions as there are points. The 2 points for air-pressure vocabulary could be two multiple-choice questions, two true/false questions, two fill-in-the-blank questions, or a combination of these different types of questions. There could even be one 2-point question, although that would not be likely for vocabulary recall. The 3 points for identifying what causes wind direction and speed could be three multiple-choice or other 1-point questions, or one 3-point constructed-response question. You would write or select the questions that best sample the knowledge and skills described by the blueprint.

EXAMPLE OF A PERFORMANCE ASSESSMENT BLUEPRINT. A 6th grade teacher, working with the Common Core State Standards, had worked with students on the concept of author's purpose, using several different texts. Learning targets and their associated performances of understanding had helped students learn about several ways in which authors communicate to readers. Figure 8.4 (p. 142) shows the standards the teacher addressed and the general learning targets she used to teach them, organized into a blueprint for a performance assessment to be used as a summative assessment (i.e., for a grade) .

The daily learning targets would have been specific to the performance of understanding, not stated generally as they are here. For example, the learning target "I can explain how a written piece is organized and why the author might have organized it that way" might have been taught over several lessons. Each lesson would have had a specific target ("I can explain how [author] organized [text] and give reasons why [s/he] might have done it that way").

The teacher selects an idea for a performance assessment task suggested in the Common Core State Standards materials (Common Core State Standards Initiative, 2010):

8.4 Example of a Performance Assessment Blueprint for a 6th Grade Reading of Informational Text

Outline	Total Points	%
Integration of Knowledge and Ideas • I can tell how the author meant to affect readers by evaluating how s/he used language and presented information. [Two 4-point rubrics, one for the thesis statement and one for the quality of reasoning/explanation]	8	50
Craft and Structure • I can explain the author's purpose for writing a piece. [4-point rubric]	4	25
Key Ideas and Details • I can support my ideas about a written piece with details from the text. [4-point rubric]	4	25
Total	16	100%

> Students evaluate Jim Murphy's *The Great Fire* to identify which aspects of the text (e.g., loaded language and the inclusion of particular facts) reveal his purpose: presenting Chicago as a city that was "ready to burn." (p. 100)

She could also have used her own idea, as long as the task tapped the learning targets she listed on the blueprint. It is important that the text is one they have not discussed as a class, so that students have to do their own thinking and not just recall other discussions.

The teacher's next step is to prepare the performance task for the students. The task will present the question they have to answer, give them access to the text, and include the rubrics on which their work will be evaluated. In this example, the blueprint specifies 4-point rubrics (Advanced, Proficient, Basic, and Below Basic) on each of four different criteria:

• The thesis (conclusion about the author's use of language and information to convey his purpose);

- The quality of the explanation and reasoning;
- Understanding of author's purpose; and
- Use of supporting details from the text.

These rubrics should be written in a general form so that they don't give away answers and can be shared with students at the time the performance assessment is given.

Notice that the blueprint enables the teacher to put the intended learning targets together and take stock of the whole. It also allows her to plan the scoring so that the grade for the summative assessment keeps all aspects of the intended learning in balance. If you are using standards-based grading, the blueprint would allow you to identify achievement of several different standards with one assessment, recording achievement of each separately. Finally, we want to emphasize again that the percentages are *not* the grades you will record; the performance levels are what you will record. The percentages are simply a tool for you, the designer of the assessment, to make sure the proportions are what you intend.

REPORT CARD GRADES

Report card grades that accurately summarize achievement over a set of learning goals must start with a set of ingredients—that is, individual summative assessments —that each accurately summarizes achievement of intended learning goals. Assembling the ingredients was the point of the previous section.

To make an omelet, you need eggs. To make a *good* omelet, you need to put the eggs and other ingredients together and cook them properly. Report card grades that accurately summarize achievement of learning goals must combine the component grades in ways that maintain the intended meaning about student achievement. In this section, we briefly describe how to do this, emphasizing the role students' learning targets and performances of understanding play in your thinking. For a more complete treatment of grading methods, see Brookhart (2011) and O'Connor (2009).

HAVE A GRADING PLAN THAT FAITHFULLY REPRESENTS THE SET OF LEARNING GOALS ON WHICH YOU NEED TO REPORT. On most report cards, academic achievement is reported in one of two ways: either as a list of subjects (e.g., reading, mathematics, and science) or as a list of standards within subjects (e.g., "Understands and uses different skills and strategies to read" and "Understands the meaning of what is read").

In either case, the subject or standard represents a domain of achievement that is larger than, but contains, the domain described by the learning targets and assessed with your summative assessments. The idea is to select, from the choices available in the grading scale on which achievement is reported, the symbol (usually a number, letter, or category) that best represents student achievement in that subject or on that standard. You have information from each of the summative assessments (the "ingredients" for the report card grade), and your task is to summarize that information in such a way as to be able to report the best representation of the student's achievement.

If you summarize the information well, you will see that there is a direct link from the learning targets to the report card grades. The learning targets were the basis for learning in classroom lessons, and the performances of understanding yielded formative assessment information for improvement. At some point, you took stock of what had been learned with a summative assessment, using a blueprint that cross-referenced the grades on individual assessments with reporting standards and learning targets. Now, you summarize those individual assessment grades in ways that maintain your intended balance of information about student achievement of the content and thinking skills assessed.

The following two sections offer some guidelines to help you summarize individual assessment grades into a report card grade that is faithful to your learning targets and standards. These guidelines are brief—just enough to show that you need to be vigilant when aggregating grades to avoid unintentionally subverting the meaning you intend your grades to convey. The final grade can stay true to the underlying learning targets only if you pay attention to how you summarize the individual grades. For more direction on grading methods, see Brookhart (2011) and O'Connor (2009).

PUT GRADES ON COMPARABLE SCALES WITH MEANINGFUL PERFORMANCE LEVELS. If the grades from your individual summative assessments are not on the same scale, the properties of the scales will alter the final information. We call it "arithmetic injustice" when a teacher puts two scales together whose numbers or levels behave differently and gets a final result that isn't what she intended. When you record your grades, put them all on the same scale. We recommend the performance scale that matches your reporting scale, if possible. For example, you might record whether a student is Advanced, Proficient, Basic, or Below Basic on each summative assessment. Or you might record whether the student's performance was at the *A, B, C, D,* or *F* level for each summative assessment. If you have a test that results in a percentage correct (say, 82%) and a project that is graded with rubrics (perhaps with four 4-point criteria), don't record these noncomparable numbers. Instead, translate students' performance on each into the same scale, and record those. Then, when you summarize, you'll be comparing apples to apples.

Some district grading policies require percentages for the report card grades themselves. We are not enthusiastic about this practice, because it lends itself to misuses of rubrics. However, if percentages are required, follow the same guideline: record all grades in the percent scale. To make those percentages meaningful, however, make sure all the point scales on which they are based are long enough. If rubrics lead to too few "points," the percentages won't mean what you want them to mean. For example, "percenting" a 4, 3, 2, 1 rubric results in 100, 75, 50, 25, with no options in between. The same holds true for a quiz with just a few questions.

Also, be careful of how you handle failing grades and zeros (Reeves, 2004). Because the F range in a percentage scale is so much bigger than all the other grade ranges, a low grade in one assessment may end up contributing more to the final grade than the other summative assessments, even if that was not the intent.

COMBINE GRADES IN A WAY THAT MAINTAINS THE PERFORMANCE-LEVEL MEANING. Once you have all your summative assessment (achievement) grades recorded on the same scale, it's time to combine them into a summary grade. A blueprint-like grading plan is helpful here because it shows you how much weight to give each summative assessment. Use the standards and learning targets to think through the weighting. Which learning targets were more important? On which learning targets did you spend more time? Those should carry more weight in the final grade.

After weighting the individual "ingredient" grades so that they contribute more or less heavily to the final grade, as you intended, summarize them into one grade by taking the median of the individual grades. In most circumstances, the median will be a better representation of typical performance on a standard than the more familiar mean (sometimes called the "average").

But don't stop there! Remember, your task is *not* to do a set of calculations on your class grades. Your task is to select, from the choices available in the grading scale on which achievement is reported, the symbol that best represents student achievement in that subject or on that standard. The median grade will be the best representation for most—*but not all*—students.

Therefore, after you have your class list of median grades, do a "judgment review" and revise the grade in the rare cases when the median is not, in your judgment, the best representation of student achievement. There are two circumstances when the median may not be the best representation.

The first is when a student's pattern of achievement has been one of steady improvement. In that case, privilege recent evidence. Suppose, for example, that a student began a report period at Basic level on a standard, but improved so that he reliably performed at the Proficient level by the end of the report period. The median grade may be Basic, but this student's current status on that standard is Proficient. Use your judgment, based on the pattern in the achievement evidence, to revise the grade and assign Proficient.

The second circumstance is when the grade is right on the borderline between two categories. Then the question becomes, "In my judgment, does the higher or lower grade best represent this student's achievement in the subject or on the standard?" Use additional achievement evidence to answer that question. We don't mean that you should put more numbers into your calculation of the median. Rather, consider how the student did in the performances of understanding you observed. Which grade or proficiency level did the student's work, overall, reflect? Use your judgment, based on this additional evidence, to assign the appropriate grade.

LOOKING FORWARD

In this chapter, we have illustrated how keeping students' learning targets in mind leads to grading decisions that generate meaningful, interpretable grades for individual summative assessments and report cards. Throughout this book, we have applied the idea of learning targets to various aspects of formative assessment, to differentiated instruction, to higher-order thinking, and to grading. We think these are the most obvious categories of application, but we hope as you pursue your understanding and use of learning targets you will find they are useful for *every* aspect of instruction and assessment. In Chapter 9, we turn from students' learning to teachers' professional development.

9

A LEARNING TARGET THEORY OF ACTION AND EDUCATIONAL LEADERSHIP: BUILDING A CULTURE OF EVIDENCE

When you make an observation,
you have an obligation.
—M. K. Asante (2008)

Boiled down to its essence, the role of the educational leader is to make schools and classrooms work better for all students. One of the traditional ways educational leaders go about this work is to observe teaching and learning at the classroom level and use that information to improve their schools and districts. But what educational leaders *observe* depends on what they *look for*.

For example, without understanding the characteristics of a strong performance of understanding, a principal can walk through 100 classrooms each day and never notice when those characteristics are missing. That's because what an educator counts as evidence of student learning and achievement depends on what he or she believes is important and the language he or she uses to describe it (Moss, 2002). The following example from our own professional development work with schools underlines our point.

A principal in an urban high school describes an "aha moment" he had while observing an English literature lesson:

I walked into the classroom and sat down. I found the room organized and attractive. I felt that the content was important and appropriate. The teacher was passionate and captivating, and his students sat in rapt attention as he talked about the essential content for the lesson: understanding the role of the "senex figure" in Shakespeare's plays. He had a PowerPoint presentation and used the SMART Board to share important vocabulary he was using. His lecture was interesting, and he even did voices for characters. He was really into it. The lesson unfolded at a comfortable pace. Every so often he stopped and asked his students, "Are you with me?" And each time, the students would nod their heads or say, "Yes."

Suddenly, it hit me. The students quite literally were doing nothing to build understanding, try out the concept, or demonstrate whether they actually understood or could apply the concept. The teacher was the only one performing. All he required students to do was to be a faithful audience and respond in the affirmative that they were with him. There was no way he or his students had a clue whether students could identify and describe the role of the senex figure in Shakespeare's plays, or how well they could do it. There was no way to know if the students were actually learning.

Just a few months ago, I would have described the students as highly engaged. How could I have not seen this before? This time, I looked for what the students were *actually doing to pursue the learning target*. I tried to find evidence of their understanding. I couldn't! I was stunned! For me it was like that moment when the villagers realize that the emperor isn't wearing any clothes. Here was an obvious truth that I never saw before.

A SHARED THEORY OF ACTION AND A COMMON LANGUAGE

As a cohesive theory of action, learning targets bring increased clarity to the work that students, teachers, and administrators do each day to raise student achievement and increase teacher effectiveness. In a very real sense, they create a common language about what educators look for and count as evidence of effective teaching and meaningful student learning.

These shared beliefs compel action-oriented and goal-directed collaboration wherein each educator intentionally focuses his or her daily efforts on looking for and addressing inconsistencies and ineffective practices. In fact, looking for what works and what doesn't—*and doing something about it*—becomes everyone's most important work. Once educators' eyes begin to open, what they see astounds them. The following two examples illustrate this phenomenon in action.

Natalie, a middle school teacher, chuckled as she told us how the learning target theory of action caused her to notice and finally question a long-held practice. Since her first day as a teacher, she had faithfully written the instructional objectives on the board for her students:

> I would print the objectives on the board for each subject. To save time, I had permanent signs for the subjects—math, science, and so on—and beside each sign I pasted *SWBAT* in large cut-out letters. Then, all I had to do each day was write the rest of the instructional objective. It was a huge time-saver.
>
> Each year, without fail, one of my students would ask me the same question: "What's a *swah bat*?" And I would tell the student that it meant "Students will be able to." It's funny now that I finally see it. My students were trying to make sense out of instructional jargon. I was writing this stuff on the board because it was supposed to help them. But how could it help them if they couldn't understand it?

Teachers and principals aren't the only ones compelled to make a change when conditions for learning aren't right. A curriculum specialist describes a conversation she had with a retired kindergarten teacher who regularly substituted in her district:

> She stopped me in the parking lot to tell me what had happened during the first lesson of the day. She opened the lesson by directing students to practice printing their spelling words. She told them, "As soon as you get your piece of paper, begin copying your spelling words neatly from your workbook." That's when 6-year-old Oliver stopped her and said, "You forgot to give us our learning target and 'I can' statements. Our teacher says we can't keep an eye on our work if we aren't sure what we're aiming for."

As the curriculum director put it, here was solid evidence that students are able to take ownership of their own learning: "If the kindergarten class can do this, there is no excuse for the rest of the students in our district. I decided that day to push harder to make learning targets integral to what happens in every lesson in our district."

ARE WE LOOKING FOR WHAT ACTUALLY WORKS?

Picture the typical list of educational "best practices." The lists are normally saturated with descriptions of what teachers do—the instructional methods, strategies, and techniques someone deemed "best." Traditionally, principals use these lists as "look-fors": techniques administrators are supposed to see, describe, and evaluate as they walk through a classroom or conduct a formal observation. Ultimately, leaders are supposed to use the information they gather from their observations as feedback to help teachers to improve the quality of their instruction and raise student achievement.

The problem with this setup is obvious. A traditional list of best-practice look-fors asks the principal to gather frequent "snapshots" of teacher actions, including how well the teacher differentiates the lesson, integrates technology, manages the classroom, uses specific instructional strategies, and provides academic rigor. Even when these forms and structures invite principals to describe what *students* are doing, they are directed to look for something called "student engagement"—a concept that has become so diluted and ubiquitous that it is nearly meaningless. Ask a thousand principals to define *student engagement,* and you will hear a thousand individual theories, most having something to do with students being "on task." Unfortunately, too few principals ask the jugular question: "Engaged in what?" Students may be working feverishly on a task that is meaningless.

Here's the bottom line: what principals "look for" in the classroom is exactly what they see, and what they will continue to see. That's because teachers will continue to demonstrate the behaviors and practices that they know their principals are looking for.

WHAT WE EVALUATE IS WHAT WE PERPETUATE

What we evaluate is quite literally where we place value—what we deem to have worth. A culture identifies certain actions and conditions as significant to its success, and members of the culture assess the extent to which these things are in place.

What members of a district look for during classroom observations signifies what they value and communicates the culture of their district. For that reason, what educational leaders actually do, more than what they say, influences what is accepted as strong evidence of student achievement. If the leadership team focuses exclusively on data from standardized test scores and audits of teachers' actions and decisions, then instructional methods and standardized test scores will continue to be the coin of the realm—the way everyone in the building measures what is valued.

In too many cases, classroom observations are audits of teacher performance. Information on instructional decisions is valuable, and we are not discounting it. But details about what the teacher is doing tell only half the story of what is and isn't working in the classroom. The rest of the story—the more significant part—is told through what students are doing and the evidence they produce while they are doing it.

If the leadership team places increased value on what students are doing during a lesson, then a transformational value system will begin to take root. Once the leadership team adopts and communicates a learning target theory of action, it can use every opportunity to learn more about what students are actually doing during today's lesson to increase their understanding, produce evidence of their learning, and raise their achievement. Although educational leaders will still observe teaching behaviors, they will do so from a decidedly different point of view.

At the end of this chapter, we share useful strategies that help school leaders place greater emphasis on learning targets and high-quality evidence of student learning. To put those strategies in context, in the following section we review what research says about the influence of educational leadership on student achievement.

EDUCATIONAL LEADERSHIP: THE CATALYST FOR STUDENT ACHIEVEMENT

When researchers (Leithwood, Louis, Anderson, & Wahlstrom, 2004) examined the links between student achievement and educational leadership practices, they found that leadership is second only to classroom instruction among all school-related factors that contribute to student learning. What's more, the contribution of effective leadership is largest when it is needed most. There are virtually no documented instances of turning a troubled school around without intervention from talented leaders. Although many factors must work in unison to transform an underperforming learning environment, leadership is clearly the catalyst.

A learning target theory of action can better equip educational leaders to exercise vigilance over instruction and support an effective learning environment. It makes them better able to conduct strategic observations, provide targeted feedback to teachers, and forge strong learning partnerships between teachers and students (Augustine et al., 2009; Moss et al., 2011a, 2011b).

The Role of Educational Leadership

Look beyond the walls and test scores of an excellent school district or building, and you will find excellent educational leadership. What we know about excellent leaders is that they have significant effects on student learning, second only to the effects of teacher expertise and quality of the curriculum. We know that school leadership is most successful when it is focused on teaching and learning (Leithwood & Riehl, 2003). It makes sense, then, that effective leaders play a crucial role in high-quality schools (Darling-Hammond, LaPointe, Meyerson, Orr, & Cohen, 2007), because they spend more quality time in the classroom (National College for School Leadership, 2007).

To capture the need for leaders to place teaching and learning at the forefront of the decisions they make, the educational community coined the term *instructional leadership*. This phrase has been in vogue for decades, and its overuse means that it often functions as an empty slogan. Simply encouraging someone to be an instructional leader is no more meaningful than cautioning the CEO of any organization to keep her eye on the organizational "ball" (Leithwood, 2007).

Lately, the term *data-driven decision maker* has added another layer to what we expect from an instructional leader. In today's standards-driven landscape of accountability, educational leaders are encouraged to collect, organize, and analyze data using innovative software packages that store, share, and compare mountains of data in ways that would have been impractical just a few years ago. Two important cautions regarding data-driven decision making are worth mentioning here.

1. **Data from standardized tests are not educational goals.** The data we collect are not "ends," or the reason for doing what we do as educators. They are means—and not the sole means—that we use to improve student achievement and increase teacher effectiveness. Standardized test scores are the signposts we consult periodically during our journey. They are useful markers that can tell us some things about our journey, but they are neither the journey nor the destination. In fact, if we think about standardized tests as large directional signposts, then learning targets and success criteria are the mile markers that help students, teachers, and principals figure out exactly where they are relative to where they need to be and assess their progress minute by minute during today's lesson.

2. **All data are not created equal.** Standardized tests happen too infrequently to be the sole data source of decisions about how to raise student achievement and improve teacher effectiveness. The decisions that matter most are the

ones made by the students themselves in partnership with their teacher during each lesson. Standardized test scores *always* give an incomplete picture of what is happening in the classroom. A learning target theory of action, on the other hand, reveals exactly what is working during a lesson and what isn't. It provides living, breathing indicators that we can use to assess collaborative, targeted, and goal-driven action.

The Principal as a Formative Leader

Much literature on successful leadership practices supports what we are learning about formative leaders. It underscores our belief that consistent, well-informed support from educational leaders in general, and the principal in particular, can have a significant influence on student achievement (Hallinger, 2005; Mosenthal, Lipson, Torncello, Russ, & Mekkelson, 2004).

Research tells us that when principals engage in targeted professional development—specifically, in interactions with teachers about improving what happens in the classroom—their leadership is more likely to positively affect teaching and learning (Brookhart et al., 2011; Camburn, Rowan, & Taylor, 2003; Moss et al., 2011a, 2011b). In fact, developing principals' ability to provide formative feedback to improve classroom practices can be more important than deepening their specific content knowledge (Spillane, Hallett, & Diamond, 2003). This is especially true in middle and secondary schools, where the realities of multiple disciplines make it highly unlikely that a principal can provide expert content support for each teacher and each subject. What's more important is to develop principals who ensure that strategic instructional practices that raise student achievement are embedded in each lesson (City, Elmore, Fiarman, & Teitel, 2009; Halverson, Grigg, Prichett, & Thomas, 2007; Louis, Leithwood, Wahlstrom, & Anderson, 2010; Silins & Mulford, 2004).

Principals who are able to engage in formative and generative professional discourse with teachers about how to refine teachers' instructional practices to raise student achievement are principals who see themselves as competent to do so. We refer to this sense of confidence as *positive self-efficacy,* and research tells us that leaders who measure high in positive self-efficacy perform much better in leadership situations than do their less-confident counterparts (Chemers, Watson, & May, 2000). What's more, leaders with high levels of positive self-efficacy tend to be part of leadership teams that exhibit high levels of positive collective efficacy—confidence in one another's competence and in team members' combined ability to be successful. It's no wonder that multiple researchers point to positive self-efficacy as a key variable in understanding how leaders regulate themselves in dynamic educational environments (McCormick, 2001). District practices, including the kind of support that districts provide to principals, can influence collective efficacy within a district (Zaccaro, Blair, Peterson, & Zazanis, 1995).

In 2001, the National Conference of State Legislatures convened a task force that examined school leadership's influence on student achievement. The task force's report summarized an 18-month investigation of exemplary principals and schools and policy options that focus on school leadership. The task force emphasized that continually providing targeted professional development is essential to ensuring that school leaders possess the necessary knowledge and skills they need to influence student achievement, specifically in the areas of student assessment, application of data, instructional leadership, and curriculum (National Conference of State Legislatures, 2002). In other words, efforts to raise student achievement must be matched by efforts to raise leadership effectiveness.

Achievement of What?

Aiming for achievement means that you are looking for evidence of something. A learning target theory of action makes that "something," in today's lesson and every lesson, public and visible. In our work with schools, we have found that educational leaders play a pivotal role in the conceptual shift promoted by this theory of action. Formative leadership can move a district from a focus on teacher-centered instructional objectives to a focus on learning targets and success criteria that both students and adults use to understand, assess, and advance their own learning. Indeed, our experience and the experiences of the educational leaders we are privileged to work with tell us that this conceptual shift is a game changer.

For this conceptual shift to take root, three layers of change must take place.

LAYER 1: TO LEAD THEIR SCHOOLS USING A LEARNING TARGET THEORY OF ACTION, ADMINISTRATORS MUST ASSUME THE ROLE OF THE LEADING LEARNER. Our theory of action promotes a learning-focused rather than an instruction-focused school culture. In a learning-focused culture, the adults in the school see themselves as intentional learners who view their buildings and classrooms as living laboratories in which they increase their knowledge and skill to foster student learning. The educational administrator functions as the principal learner, leading the learning of students, teachers, administrators, staff, and members of the school community (Moss & Brookhart, 2009). We use the term *culture* to describe the shared beliefs, norms, and artifacts of a particular group of people (Johnson & Christensen,

2012). Learning targets promote a cultural change from teacher-centered, evaluative beliefs and normative practices to a collective theory of action that centers on what students believe and know and uses what students are actually doing to learn as the standard. That cultural change can't happen in only one classroom in a building.

The culture of a building or a district doesn't change without its leaders. Administrators need to lead by example, provide feedback that feeds forward, see themselves as the leading learners in the district, and treat teachers as co-learners. That's why our learning target theory of action promotes a culture of collaborative learning in which administrators, teachers, and students "co-labor"—work together—to raise student achievement.

LAYER 2: TO COMMIT TO A LEARNING TARGET THEORY OF ACTION, ADMINISTRATORS NEED TO LOOK FOR AND ANALYZE WHAT STUDENTS ARE ACTUALLY DOING AND LEARNING IN THEIR BUILDINGS' CLASSROOMS. Evidence of student learning helps leaders analyze what is working in their districts, lesson by lesson and for specific teachers, groups of teachers, or buildings. As administrators sharpen their focus on learning targets, they ramp up their own professional learning and commitment by recognizing what students are being asked to do to learn and produce evidence of their achievement. This focus contrasts with the more conventional supervisor's visit to a classroom to observe teaching behavior. During the traditional observation, administrators audit "student engagement"—usually defined as being busy and complying with a teacher's requests.

If school leaders want teachers to adopt a learning target theory of action, they must intentionally learn about it, commit to it, and model it themselves. They must critique their own ability to use specific, learning-focused language to describe what teachers are doing well, identify the next steps teachers should take to increase their effectiveness, and provide feed-forward information to teachers while they still have time to act on it. In this way, they help teachers set more challenging short-term and long-range goals that benefit all students.

LAYER 3: TO KNOW WHAT TO LOOK FOR AND ANALYZE IN CLASSROOMS, ADMINISTRATORS NEED TO UNDERSTAND A LEARNING TARGET THEORY OF ACTION AT A DEEP LEVEL THEMSELVES. To support a learning target theory of action, administrators need to be especially skillful at observing students working and interpreting what's going on with their learning. Is what they are doing leading to increased understanding and producing compelling evidence of that understanding? As leading learners, school leaders should be partnering with teachers to look for and share examples of expert teaching that positively affects student learning.

In other words, before educational leaders can promote a learning target theory of action, they must make the shift themselves, clarifying their own view of what they accept as evidence that all students are learning and achieving to their potential.

ACTION TOOLS AND CULTURE-BUILDING STRATEGIES

It takes intentional, cohesive, and incremental effort to develop an evidence-based culture and a common language based on a learning target theory of action. Meaningful change doesn't happen overnight, and it doesn't happen for all teachers, students, and principals at the same pace. It takes courage and persistence to call into question educational practices that were once blindly accepted. It takes commitment and collaboration to develop an increasingly sophisticated common language that describes student learning as the achievement of appropriate and challenging learning targets.

What follows is our explanation of action tools and strategies that we have developed in our continued professional development work with teachers, administrators, and school districts. What makes them particularly powerful is that they support assessing practice against specific criteria *and* using specific evidence to justify each claim for meeting performance criteria.

Action Tool A: Understanding Learning Targets

Educators often struggle with the concept of learning targets because of an all-too-common misconception: they equate a learning target with an instructional objective. Understanding the distinction between an instructional objective and a high-quality learning target for today's lesson is crucial. The examples provided in this action tool are written at the elementary school level and use easily understood lesson concepts, enabling educators to focus on the attributes of a learning target in a familiar context.

Use this action tool to help individual educators and groups of educators deepen their understanding of what learning targets are and, even more important, what they are not. Teachers can examine the learning targets they design against the definitions and checklist provided in this action tool.

Action Tool B: Learning Target Classroom Walk-Through Guide

Helping principals and other educational leaders recognize and understand the fusion of learning targets, success criteria, a strong performance of understanding, and feedback that feeds forward is a great way to begin this professional development work.

The Learning Target Classroom Walk-Through Guide helps school leaders learn to look for and analyze what is actually happening during today's lesson. Leaders can use the guide as an observational framework during a classroom visit, or after a classroom visit to summarize the evidence they collected and analyze what it means for student achievement.

One especially powerful way to use the walk-through guide is as a framework for professional development. Have each member of the leadership team visit a classroom and record what he or she observed using the guide. As a learning team, analyze and discuss the patterns that emerge across individual observations and insights. Then plan next steps that the leadership team will take on the basis of its observations. The plan should include action steps for further skill building and professional learning based on the gaps and challenges revealed through your observations and discussions.

Action Tool C: Learning Target Lesson-Planning Process Guide

Moving from instructional objectives to learning targets is a process that requires planning, practice, and self-assessment. A great way to build a culture of shared understanding is to use the Learning Target Lesson-Planning Process Guide to develop teacher understanding and expertise. We have used this process in a number of ways, including the following:

- **Break the process guide into increasingly challenging chunks.** For example, start out by moving from using an instructional objective, to identifying the essential content and reasoning processes of the instructional objective that are the focus of today's lesson, to designing the learning target and the performance of understanding. When you develop proficiency with these steps, add reasonably challenging next steps of the process to continue to build understanding and expertise.
- **Form a professional learning community around learning targets.** Ask teachers from the same grade or subject area to work through an upcoming lesson together, teach the lesson, and then reflect on what went well and where they should set goals for their professional improvement efforts. Use chunks of the guide (as suggested above) to increase the level of challenge and the level of professional achievement.
- **Form administrator-teacher learning teams.** Use the process guide together. The teacher serves as the content expert and plans an upcoming lesson with

the administrator, discussing each step together, questioning understanding, and justifying decisions. Then the teacher can use the plan to actually teach the lesson while the administrator "sits in" to learn how the plan works and consider which next steps to take with the teacher to learn more about the process. After the lesson, the teacher and the administrator discuss what teaching and learning were visible and what was missing.

Action Tool D: Teacher Self-Assessment Targets and Look-Fors Guide

A learning target theory of action means that even the adults in the school must learn to set mastery goals and use specific criteria to assess their progress toward those goals. This guide details for teachers and administrators what effective teaching and empowered learning look like in today's lesson. Use this guide in conjunction with the other action tools to deepen understanding, increase the accuracy of your professional goals, and maximize opportunities to feed forward one another's learning. Teachers can use the guide independently to reflect on their own practice, in learning teams to collaborate on professional improvement efforts, or as a way to collect and organize artifacts for teaching portfolios.

Action Tool E: Student Self-Assessment and Intentional Learning Guide

A learning target theory of action requires all members of the school—teachers, administrators, and students—to assess their progress toward visible learning targets. This guide is explicitly designed to mirror the decisions that assessment-capable students make and the actions they take throughout the formative learning cycle. The guide helps students (1) aim for the learning target; (2) know where they are in relation to it; (3) set goals for what they need to do to close the gap; (4) seek clarity by asking effective questions; and (5) select specific learning strategies that will help them get to where they need to go. Students learn to make informed decisions about improving their own learning during today's lesson.

You can use this action tool during each phase of the formative learning cycle. Consider providing students with a new copy of the guide after each phase of the formative learning cycle. This way, they can chart their progress throughout the lesson and become more detailed in describing their decisions and actions. After each phase, ask students to reflect on where they are and where they need to be. Once students become accustomed to thinking about and approaching their work in this way, they can use one copy of the guide to chart their progress during an entire lesson.

Action Tool F: No More "Garbage In, Garbage Out": Understanding Connections Among Instruction, Assessment, and Grading

The phrase "garbage in, garbage out" (GIGO) originated in the computer science and mathematics world. This concise metaphor reminds us that if you input incorrect or weak data, your results will also be incorrect or weak. This concept carries across numerous contexts. For example, if you prepare a meal using incorrect or poor-quality ingredients, don't expect to serve a high-quality meal. In cooking as well as in grading, it pays to ensure that something is of good quality before you use it.

This action tool explains the relationship among learning targets, effective instruction, meaningful student learning, strong evidence of student achievement, and grading. First and foremost, all students should receive high-quality instruction that engages them in performances of understanding during which they aim for important learning targets. Second, students' grades should be based on the same learning targets that students were asked to aim for during the lessons. It makes no sense to ask students to learn one thing and then grade them on another. Keeping students' learning targets in mind during the grading process produces meaningful, interpretable grades for individual summative assessments and report cards. A learning target theory of action builds a culture of evidence in which all educators adopt a grading stance anchored by the belief that academic grades should be based on achievement of learning goals.

Use this action tool to prompt discussions about the importance of providing high-quality learning experiences in every lesson. Focus on the influence that learning targets, success criteria, and a performance of understanding in today's lesson can have on the evidence that teachers use to summarize learning. Begin the discussion by asking the two questions that appear on the first page of the action tool. Then use the big ideas and accompanying graphic organizers to focus the relationship between a learning target theory of action and summative assessments and grades that are truly representative of student achievement.

Expanding the Culture of Evidence: Partnering with Parents and Family

Learning targets and success criteria offer an especially useful way to communicate with students' parents or other caregivers. Often, the communication parents receive from the school arrives as grades, teacher comments on student assignments, or report cards. Or it takes the form of a prepared newsletter that shares general announcements, overarching educational goals, and schoolwide achievements. These communications do little to help parents focus on what students are actually doing during daily lessons to learn and achieve important concepts and skills.

Sharing learning targets with parents forges an extended learning partnership with the home. Teachers can use "I can" statements to help parents understand what is important for their child to know and be able to do as a result of a specific lesson or group of lessons. Teachers can use "I can" statements in web pages, wikis, blogs, e-mails, letters, and hard-copy handouts.

The following example tells parents exactly what their 3rd grade children will be expected to learn during a week of social studies lessons exploring community economics.

Dear parents,

Our class is learning about the economics of our community. We are working toward the following curriculum standard: "Students will demonstrate a basic understanding of a consumer economy, including how local producers have used natural, human, and capital resources to produce goods and services in the past and the present."

One of our learning targets is to be able to explain how people and businesses create jobs when they buy goods and services from one another, and when they sell goods and services to one another.

By the end of the week, your child should be able to demonstrate his or her mastery of the target by being able to say

1. I can name people and businesses in our town who buy goods.

2. I can name people and businesses in our town who pay for services.

3. I can name people and businesses in our town who make goods and sell them.

4. I can name people and businesses in our town who provide services for money.

5. I can give examples of how the people and businesses in our town who buy goods and pay for services help create jobs.

6. I can give examples of how the people and businesses in our town who make goods and provide services help to create jobs.

You can help your child learn more about the economics of our community by discussing local businesses with your child. Help your child think about what local businesses and service providers make and purchase. Point out all the people your child knows and interacts with who have jobs in our local businesses, organizations, industries, public institutions, and agencies.

Sincerely,
Mr. Starkey's 3rd grade learning team

THE PROMISE OF A LEARNING TARGET THEORY OF ACTION

Educational cultures where collaborative, evidence-based decision making is focused by a cohesive theory of action are rarer than we think, more difficult than we think, and more promising than we think. They require bone-deep commitment and professional vigilance, both in the short term and over the long haul.

We are convinced that a learning target theory of action propels a high-leverage and generative process that continuously builds such a culture. When educators design, aim for, and gather evidence about learning targets, they make expert teaching and meaningful learning visible during today's lesson and every lesson in their classrooms and schools. At the same time, they shine a light into places where learning is stalled and teaching is ineffective. Their actions build a common language to describe what they look for as evidence of what is working to raise student achievement. Just as important, when they observe what is not working, they recognize their obligation to do something about it and take strategic steps to improve instructional quality.

In this book, we have explained a learning target theory of action that arose from our professional development work with educators who are using the theory to increase their expertise and raise student achievement. To truly benefit from this theory of action, you will need to add strategies of your own based on the evidence you gather and the goals you set with your colleagues. By combining the best of what you learn with what we share in this book, you can improve your teaching expertise and leadership effectiveness and dramatically empower all students in your care to develop as assessment-capable and self-regulated learners.

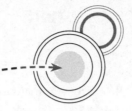

ACTION TOOLS

Download Instructions

The Action Tools in this book are available for download at www
.ascd.org/downloads.

Enter this unique key code to unlock the files: G66C7-0BB47-D5713

If you have difficulty accessing the files, e-mail webhelp@ascd.org or
call 1-800-933-ASCD for assistance.

ACTION TOOL A:
Understanding Learning Targets

What Is a Learning Target?

The most effective teaching and the most meaningful student learning happen when teachers design the right learning target for today's lesson and use it along with their students to aim for and assess understanding.

A learning target describes, in language that students understand, the lesson-sized chunk of information, skills, and reasoning processes that students will come to know deeply and thoroughly.

How Does a Learning Target Differ from an Instructional Objective?

An *instructional objective* describes an intended outcome and the nature of evidence that will determine mastery of that outcome from a teacher's point of view. It contains content outcomes, conditions, and criteria.

A *learning target* describes the intended lesson-sized learning outcome and the nature of evidence that will determine mastery of that outcome from a student's point of view. It contains the immediate learning aims for today's lesson.

	Instructional Objective— Framed from the Teacher Point of View	Learning Target— Framed from the Student Point of View
Where does it come from?	• Derived from a standard and/or curricular goal.	• Derived from an instructional objective.
Who uses it?	• Used by the teacher to guide instruction during a lesson or over a group of lessons.	• Used by the teacher and the students to aim for understanding and assess the quality of student work during today's lesson.
What does it describe, and how does it describe it?	• Describes content knowledge (concepts, understandings) and skills that students should be able to demonstrate. • Uses teacher language (the language of curriculum and standards). • May span one lesson or a set of lessons.	• Asks, "What am I going to learn?" • Uses student language as well as pictures, models, and/or demonstrations when possible. • Asks, "What should I be able to do at the end of today's lesson? And how is it connected to yesterday's and tomorrow's lessons?"
How does it connect to a performance of understanding?	• Generalizes to many potential tasks, from which teachers select one or several to be the performance of understanding for instructional activities and formative assessment for a series of lessons.	• Is connected to the specific performance of understanding that the teacher has chosen for today's lesson.
How does it promote evidence-based assessment?	• Includes criteria and performance standards in teacher language.	• Includes student look-fors—criteria and performance standards in student language—often accompanied by tools (e.g., "I can" statements, rubrics, checklists) and examples of work.

Checklist for Evaluating Learning Targets

A learning target contains ALL of the following characteristics. It must

☐ Describe exactly what the student is going to learn by the end of today's lesson.

☐ Be stated in developmentally appropriate language that the student can understand.

☐ Be framed from the point of view of a student who has not yet mastered the intended learning outcome for today's lesson.

☐ Be connected to and shared through the specific performance of understanding designed by the teacher for today's lesson (what students will be asked to do, say, make, or write that will deepen student understanding, allow students to assess where they are in relation to the learning target, and provide evidence of mastery).

☐ Include student look-fors—descriptive criteria that students can use to judge how close they are to the target, stated in terms that describe mastery of the learning target (not in terms that describe how the students' performance will be scored or graded).

Learning Targets: Helping Students Aim for Understanding in Today's Lesson
Connie M. Moss and Susan M. Brookhart [© 2012 by ASCD. All rights reserved.]

MATHEMATICS EXAMPLE	To focus and direct learning, you need:		
	Content outcome	**Conditions**	**Criteria**
	Knowledge and/or skills a student should be able to demonstrate	Circumstances under which students will be able to perform	Qualities of performance by which you will know that the student has reached desired level of learning
Teacher's instructional objective for a set of lessons focused on teaching: 3-digit addition with carrying.	The student will be able to solve problems using 3-digit addition with carrying in the ones' place.	Without using calculators or fact charts.	The student will perform with 80 percent accuracy.
	What am I going to learn?	**How will I show what I know?**	**How will I know how well I am doing—what are my look-fors?**
Students' learning target for today's lesson on: Introducing carrying.	I am going to be able to use a method called "carrying" so that I know what to do with the 10 under 8+2 or the 12 under 9+3 in problems like these: $\begin{array}{r}438\\+152\\\hline\end{array}$ $\begin{array}{r}219\\+363\\\hline\end{array}$	I will use a paper and pencil and show my work as I solve the problems.	I can explain and show how to put the carrying marks in the right places as I solve the problems (most of the time). My work will look like this example: $\begin{array}{r}2\,1\,9\\+363\\\hline 5\,8\,2\end{array}$
Students' learning target for another day's lesson on: Practicing for accuracy and proficiency.	I am going to be able to use carrying to solve problems like these accurately and smoothly: $\begin{array}{r}438\\+152\\\hline\end{array}$ $\begin{array}{r}219\\+363\\\hline\end{array}$	I will use a paper and pencil and show my work as I solve the problems.	I can put the carrying marks in the right places and use them to get the correct answers (most of the time).
Students' learning target for yet another day's lesson on: Identifying relevant problems.	I am going to be able to write my own story problems that need 3-digit addition with carrying as part of their solution.	I will create stories from my own classroom or home or shopping.	I can write three story problems that need 3-digit addition with carrying as part of their solution [depending on the lesson, may add "and I can solve them correctly"].
COUNTEREXAMPLE: NOT a learning target for today's lesson	I can do 3-digit addition with carrying in the ones' place to solve problems. [NOTE: This is not one lesson-sized chunk, and it is mostly in teacher language, just with an "I can" stuck on at the beginning.]	Without using calculators or fact charts.	I will get at least a B on my quiz. [NOTE: This criterion is about scoring, not showing learning. It is not shared as student look-for.]

Learning Targets: Helping Students Aim for Understanding in Today's Lesson
Connie M. Moss and Susan M. Brookhart

READING EXAMPLE	To focus and direct learning, you need:		
	Content outcome	Conditions	Criteria
	Knowledge and/or skills a student should be able to demonstrate	Circumstances under which students will be able to perform	Qualities of performance by which you will know that the student has reached desired level of learning
Teacher's instructional objective for a set of lessons focused on teaching: The concept of main idea.	The student will be able to identify main idea.	In grade-level-appropriate reading passages one paragraph in length.	The student can say, select, or write the main idea of a passage with 80 percent accuracy.
	What am I going to learn?	How will I show what I know?	How will I know how well I am doing—what are my look-fors?
Students' learning target for today's lesson on: Identifying the main idea of a paragraph.	I will learn that a main idea is the most important thing the writer of a paragraph is trying to tell me.	I will read paragraphs and choose the main idea for each paragraph from a list.	I can choose the right main idea and explain why it was more important than the other choices.
Students' learning target for another day's lesson on: Summarizing main ideas that are stated literally.	I will learn to answer the question "What does the writer say is the main idea?" in one sentence.	I will read paragraphs and look for main ideas that the author has stated. I will usually find these in the topic sentence.	I can restate the paragraph's main idea in my own words, in one sentence.
Students' learning target for yet another day's lesson on: Making inferences to identify the main idea.	I will learn to answer the question "What is the writer trying to tell me?" in one sentence.	I will read a paragraph, think about how all the details in the paragraph are related, and describe what the paragraph as a whole is trying to say.	I can summarize the paragraph's main idea in my own words, in one sentence.
COUNTEREXAMPLE: NOT a learning target for today's lesson	I can identify the main idea in a paragraph. [NOTE: This is not one lesson-sized chunk, and it is mostly in teacher language, just with an "I can" stuck on at the beginning.]	I will read a paragraph. [NOTE: This is too general. It is not connected to a specific performance of understanding.]	I will get all of the teacher's main idea questions right. [NOTE: This criterion is about scoring, not showing learning. It is also too general and cannot serve as a student look-for that promotes meaningful self-assessment.]

Learning Targets: Helping Students Aim for Understanding in Today's Lesson
Connie M. Moss and Susan M. Brookhart

ACTION TOOL B:
Learning Target Classroom Walk-Through Guide

PURPOSE: To help school leaders "look for," recognize, and analyze what is actually happening in today's lesson to promote effective teaching, meaningful learning, and increased student achievement.

Suggestions for Use

- **For an individual school leader:** Use the action tool to focus a walk-through or classroom visit or as a reflective framework to begin a formative conversation with the teacher about the observation.
- **For a professional learning community of school leaders:** Each leader performs an analysis of a classroom visit using the entire action tool or part of it, depending on the learning focus. Then leaders compare, discuss, and analyze their findings as individuals and as a leadership team. Use findings to plan for long-term and short-term professional learning goals and professional development opportunities for teachers and school leaders.

Directions

Use the checklist to focus your observation on what students are *actually* doing during today's lesson to aim for understanding and what the teacher is doing to help them achieve. The checklist focuses on the relationship among the three essential elements of a formative learning cycle: the learning target and success criteria, the performance of understanding, and feedback that feeds learning forward. Only when these relationships are in place are you operating with a learning target theory of action.

LEARNING TARGET: A description of what the student is going to learn by the end of today's lesson, stated in developmentally appropriate language that the student can understand and aim for during today's lesson. Learning target language is framed from the point of view of a student who has not yet mastered the target and includes student look-fors—criteria that students can use to judge how close they are to the target, stated in language that describes mastery rather than grading or scoring. The learning target is connected to the specific performance of understanding for today's lesson.

STUDENT LOOK-FORS: A student-friendly term that teachers use to describe success criteria. Look-fors are stated in feed-forward language that sets students up to use the criteria for self-assessment, self-regulation, and goal setting.

SUCCESS CRITERIA: Descriptions of what it means to do quality work in today's lesson in terms that are lesson-sized, observable, and measurable, so that students can use them to assess the quality of their work while they are learning. The criteria explain what good work (success) looks like for today's lesson to help students understand what they will be asked to do to demonstrate their learning and how well they will be asked to do it. Success criteria are specific to the learning target, understandable, and visible.

PERFORMANCE OF UNDERSTANDING: A learning experience or task that requires students to actually do, say, write, or make something during today's lesson to aim for the target, apply the success criteria, deepen their understanding, and produce compelling evidence of what they know and can do related to the target.

FEEDBACK THAT FEEDS FORWARD: Feedback that compares student work with the learning target for the lesson, describes student thinking, suggests a specific strategy for next steps, arrives during the performance of understanding (or as close to it as possible), and uses student-friendly, developmentally appropriate language.

Learning Target Classroom Walk-Through Guide

Principal's name: _____

Grade level: _____ Duration of lesson (hours/minutes): _____

Subject: _____ Topic: _____

1. **Did you see evidence that the teacher had a learning target for this specific lesson (not a learning target for a series of lessons)?**

   ☐ **Yes, I saw evidence that the teacher had a specific learning target** for today's lesson—a statement of what the students would be able to do or come to know as a result of today's lesson.

   ☐ **No. However, I saw evidence that the teacher had an instructional objective** that was used to guide teaching and that could have covered more than one lesson.

   ☐ **No, I could not find evidence that the teacher had a learning target** for the lesson, nor was there evidence of an instructional objective.

   Describe what you observed—the evidence you gathered to support your response:

2. **What did you actually see the students do, say, write, or make during today's lesson? Did you find evidence that the lesson included a strong performance of understanding?** In other words, if the students completed everything that the teacher asked them to do, would you have compelling evidence that the students had achieved the learning target for today's lesson?

   ☐ **Definitely!** The teacher asked the students to engage in an activity that deepened their understanding of the learning target's essential content and skills, encouraged students to use reasoning, required them to apply the success criteria to their own work, and produced compelling evidence of where students were in relation to the learning target.

   ☐ **Basically.** The teacher asked students to engage in an activity that was related to the learning target but produced only general evidence of where students were in relation to the learning target.

   ☐ **No.** The students were engaged in an activity, but it was not a performance of understanding. The teacher asked students to engage in an activity that was either unrelated to the learning target or produced little evidence of where students were in relation to the learning target.

   Describe what you observed—the evidence you gathered to support your response:

3. In addition to looking for a strong performance of understanding, did you see evidence that the teacher shared the learning target for the lesson with the students in any of the following additional ways?

Check all that apply. Below each item checked, describe exactly what you observed—the evidence you gathered to support your choices.

☐ The teacher shared the target verbally.

☐ The teacher asked students to put the target into their own words or explain the target to a friend.

☐ The teacher used a visual (picture, chart, SMART Board, or student handout).

☐ The teacher referred to the learning target throughout the lesson, helping students self-assess.

☐ The teacher shared examples of strong and weak work and gave students the chance to examine the characteristics of each.

☐ The teacher connected what the class was doing in today's lesson to what came before today's lesson and to what would be coming next in the unit.

4. Did you see evidence that the teacher shared student look-fors, or criteria for success, with students?

Check all that apply. Below each item checked, describe exactly what you observed—the evidence you gathered to support your choices.

☐ The teacher posted what students should look for in their work, phrased as simple, understandable "I can" statements.

☐ The teacher provided the students with a checklist of important elements for them to look for in their work. Students were given time to use the checklist.

☐ The teacher provided the students with a rubric that included both criteria and performance-level descriptions to look for in their work. Students were given a strategy for doing this (e.g., using highlighters, making notes on the rubric) and were given time to do it.

☐ The teacher co-constructed with students a rubric that included both criteria and performance-level descriptions to look for in their work. Students were given a strategy for doing this (e.g., using highlighters, making notes on the rubric) and were given time to do it.

☐ The teacher used examples of strong and weak work for students to use as comparisons with their own. (The examples could be on paper or, for performances, provided via demonstrations or modeling.) Students were given a strategy for comparing their work with the examples or models (e.g., using a rubric) and were given time to do it.

☐ The teacher organized qualities of good work into a series of questions to guide students' reasoning about the quality of their work (e.g., Do I have a strong thesis sentence that is worth writing about? Do I give more than one reason why my thesis is important?). The questions were available to students (e.g., on paper handouts or on the board), and students had time to consider and answer them.

5. Did you observe the teacher feeding students' learning forward during today's lesson? Did the teacher provide information that was timely, descriptive, and directly related to the learning target; describe where students were in relation to the success criteria; and suggest a strategy for success?

Check all that apply. Below each item checked, describe exactly what you observed—the evidence you gathered to support your choices.

☐ The teacher consistently provided feed-forward information that was related to the learning target and success criteria, described student thinking against the criteria, and suggested what students could do to improve.

☐ The teacher fed students' learning forward during the introductory part of the lesson, modeled and explained what was important to learn and be able to do, and described or demonstrated specific strategies for doing so.

☐ The teacher helped students set goals for the performance of understanding (what they would be asked to do to deepen understanding and demonstrate learning and how well they would have to do it).

☐ The teacher referred to the learning target and student look-fors during guided practice.

☐ As the teacher described what students would be asked to do during the performance of understanding, he or she explained specific strategies related to the learning target that students could use to improve their work.

☐ The teacher used written, verbal, or modeling feedback to close the gaps in understanding and/or skill that were discovered during the performance of understanding.

☐ The teacher chose the appropriate audience (an individual student, a group of students, or the entire class) to deliver feedback that was specific to those students' needs and strengths.

☐ The teacher provided an immediate opportunity for students to use the feedback (e.g., time for revision, another similar performance of understanding).

ACTION TOOL C:
Learning Target Lesson-Planning Process Guide

Purpose: To help educators move from a traditional planning process guided by an instructional objective to one guided by a learning target.

Suggestions for Use

- **For an individual teacher who wants to plan a lesson:** Use the guide to find and state the learning target. Then, with the target as your reference, create the success criteria, design a strong performance of understanding, plan other ways to share the target throughout the lesson, and recognize opportunities to feed learning forward.
- **For an individual teacher who wants to refine skills:** Use specific sections to reach a higher level of sophistication in your planning process. As you become more proficient, add additional sections over time until you are able to implement the process with confidence and competence.
- **For groups of teachers:** Use the guide for collaborative planning. Work through the guide together, discussing decisions along the way as you compare ideas and reach consensus.
- **For administrators:** Use the guide to frame conferences with teachers after a walk-through or an observation. Sit together and use the guide to plan a lesson or part of a lesson depending on the area where the teacher shows a need for professional growth or where the administrator would like to deepen understanding of this planning process.

Directions

Use this guide to move from an instructional objective that guides a series of lessons to a learning target that focuses the classroom learning team in today's lesson. The guide will help you plan ways to share the learning target, create student look-fors, feed learning forward, ask targeted questions, encourage student goal setting, and develop assessment-capable students. The insights you construct through this process will inform your planning for differentiating instruction, fostering higher-order thinking, summarizing student achievement, and grading.

Learning Target Lesson-Planning Process Guide

Grade level: _____ Duration of lesson (hours/minutes): _____

Subject: _____ Topic: _____

Today's lesson is part of this unit of study: _____

How many lessons in the unit? _____

Where does the lesson fall in the unit?   ☐ Beginning   ☐ Middle   ☐ End

1. List the instructional objective(s) for this unit or group of lessons:

2. List the essential learning content for today's lesson, including what students will come to know and be able to do by the end of today's lesson.

    2a. Essential knowledge. My students must learn that . . .

    2b. Essential skills. My students must be able to . . .

3. Identify the potential learning trajectory, or this lesson's "reason to live."

    3a. Where does this lesson occur in the unit or group of lessons?
    ☐ Beginning   ☐ Middle   ☐ End

3b. What have your students already learned about this concept from previous lessons?

3c. What lies ahead for your students? What will they tackle in tomorrow's lesson and the lessons that follow?

3d. What is this lesson's "reason to live"? What is absolutely essential for your students to come to know and be able to do in today's lesson to build on what they already know and to be prepared for the learning challenges that lie ahead?

4. Essential reasoning skill(s): what reasoning processes will best help your students actively construct the kind of understandings that are essential for today's lesson?

My students must learn to . . .

5. The performance of understanding:

- I can use information I gather from this performance to inform my plans for tomorrow's lesson.

- My students can use information they gather during the performance to select strategies for improvement.

This is what my students will do, say, write, or make during today's lesson to deepen their understanding and generate undeniable evidence of their learning so that my students and I can use it to assess their growing competence:

6. The learning target statement: answer the following questions from the "students'-eye view" in student-friendly, developmentally appropriate language.

6a. What will I be able to do when I've finished this lesson?

I can . . .

6b. What idea, topic, or subject is important for me to learn and understand so that I can use this information to do it? (Create a bulleted list.)

To be able to do this, I must learn and understand that . . .

6c. How will I be asked to show that I can do this, and how well will I have to do it?

I will show I can do this by . . .

7. Getting to the success criteria: for the performance of understanding in your lesson and based on the learning targets you will share with students, what will typical and not-so-typical student progress look like on the way to the learning target?

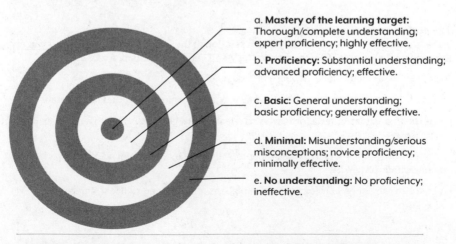

a. **Mastery of the learning target:** Thorough/complete understanding; expert proficiency; highly effective.

b. **Proficiency:** Substantial understanding; advanced proficiency; effective.

c. **Basic:** General understanding; basic proficiency; generally effective.

d. **Minimal:** Misunderstanding/serious misconceptions; novice proficiency; minimally effective.

e. **No understanding:** No proficiency; ineffective.

Learning Targets: Helping Students Aim for Understanding in Today's Lesson
Connie M. Moss and Susan M. Brookhart [© 2012 by ASCD. All rights reserved.]

7a. Describe target mastery. These students will be able to . . .

7b. Describe proficient understanding. These students are close to mastery and will be able to . . .

7c. Describe basic understanding. These students have general understanding and will be able to . . .

7d. Describe minimal understanding. These students are challenged by the content and will be confused about . . .

8. To help students assess where they are in relation to the learning target, how will you organize the criteria for success? Choose one strategy and state your reason for choosing it.

☐ An "I can" statement—for grasping a new concept or term.

☐ A list of "I can" statements to describe mastery of a learning target that is a discrete skill.

☐ A rubric to organize criteria for mastering a learning target that is part of a complex product or process.

☐ A list of student look-fors to guide students' self-assessment as they plan their work and monitor their progress.

☐ A list of guiding questions for mastery of higher-order thinking skill learning targets.

9. **In addition to engaging your students in a strong performance of understanding, how will you weave the learning target into the fabric of today's lesson to ensure that it is continuously visible? Check all that apply and explain exactly what you will do.**

☐ Verbally share the target.

What will you say or do?

☐ Ask students to paraphrase the target, put it into their own words, or explain the target to a friend to make sure they understood exactly where they are headed in today's lesson.

What will you say or do?

☐ Use a visual (e.g., a picture, a chart, SMART Board, or a student handout).

What will you say or do?

☐ Refer to the learning target throughout the lesson to help students gauge where they are in relation to the learning target.

What will you say or do?

☐ Share examples of strong and weak work and give students the chance to examine the characteristics of each to help them understand what success looks like for today's lesson.

What will you say or do?

☐ Connect what students are doing in today's lesson to what came before today's lesson and what will be coming next in the unit.

What will you say or do?

10. **Imagine the kind of mastery goal that would help two specific students during today's lesson—a student who almost gets it and one who is struggling to get it.**

10a. Finish these statements to create a "just-right goal" for a student who is close to mastery of the learning target.

I am already good at . . .

I am unsure of or confused about . . .

I need to work on this to improve my understanding:

10b. Finish these statements to create a "just-right goal" for a student who is struggling to reach the learning target. Think about common errors that students make. What would be the logical next step for the student to take?

I am already good at . . .

I am unsure of or confused about . . .

I need to work on this to improve my understanding:

11. Select, adapt, or design specific strategies that would help your two students reach their goals during the performance of understanding in today's lesson.

11a. Finish this statement to create a "just-right" next-step strategy for the student who is close to mastery of the learning target.

This is exactly what I will do:

11b. Finish this statement to create a "just-right" next-step strategy for the student who is struggling to reach the learning target. Think about common errors that students make. What would be the logical next step for the student to take?

This is exactly what I will do:

12. **Think about all the ways you can provide your students with feed-forward information during a formative learning cycle in today's lesson.**

12a. How will you plan to feed learning forward during the introductory part of the lesson, when you model and explain? Give an example of how you will use the success criteria to explain the concepts in the lesson in ways that will help students envision what mastery looks like and understand what is important to learn, what they will do to learn it, and how they will be asked to demonstrate that learning.

12b. Give an example of how you will use the learning target and success criteria to plan ways to provide feedback during guided practice.

12c. How will you use the success criteria to feed students' learning forward while you give directions for the performance of understanding?

12d. Explain how the success criteria will help you gather information during or soon after the performance of understanding to pinpoint the feedback that a particular student needs to feed his or her learning forward.

13. How will you intentionally teach and scaffold student self-assessment so that students can assess and regulate their work while they are learning during today's lesson?

13a. Finish this statement to suggest self-assessment strategies for the student who is close to mastery of the learning target. What should the student "look for" that will provide evidence of improvement?

This is how I will check my progress along the way. I will look for . . .

13b. Finish this statement to suggest self-assessment strategies for the student who is struggling to reach the learning target. Think about common errors that students make. What should the student "look for" that will provide evidence of improvement?

This is how I will check my progress along the way. I will look for . . .

14. What planned questions will you make sure to ask during today's lesson?

List five "strategic teacher questions" for today's lesson. The questions should be planned, connected to the learning target for today's lesson, and require student explanation and justification.

ACTION TOOL D:
Teacher Self-Assessment Targets and Look-Fors Guide

PURPOSE: To help teachers and school leaders reach a series of professional learning targets, assess where they are in relation to those targets, and provide detailed evidence to support their claims. This guide establishes specific success criteria by which progress toward professional goals can be assessed and monitored to aid specific goal setting and professional action plans.

Suggestions for Use

- **Administrators can use this guide in conjunction with Action Tools B and C to feed their own learning forward.** Use the guide to help you understand what specific elements of the theory look like in action in a particular lesson, classroom, grade level, school, or district.
- **Administrators can use this guide in conjunction with Action Tools B and C to feed teachers' learning forward.** Provide parts of the guide to teachers to help them focus on what it will take to master the concept of using learning targets to improve their teaching.
- **Teachers can use this guide in conjunction with Action Tools B and C to feed their own learning forward.** Use the guide to help you understand what specific elements of the theory look like in action during a particular lesson, assess your level of performance for each target, provide specific evidence to anchor your assessments, and set self-improvement goals.

Directions

The following self-assessment guide will focus your professional practice, self-reflection, and goal setting as an individual or as a professional learning community. Use the guide to reflect on your practice during a specific lesson, and notice patterns of practice that meet or do not meet a learning target theory of action. Use your findings to frame discussions with colleagues about the logical next steps you should take to increase your use of learning targets in your classroom and school. It's only through collaborative and evidence-based decision making that you will advance a learning target theory of action to improve student learning and achievement.

Teacher Self-Assessment Targets and Look-Fors Guide

Target 1: Each time I plan a lesson, I begin by defining the learning target that my students and I will aim for during that specific lesson.

I will know I have reached this target when I am able to say . . .	Not Confident	Not Very Confident	Somewhat Confident	Very Confident
• I can define the learning target for today's lesson in a clear, specific, and descriptive target statement and use it to plan my lesson.				
• I can describe exactly what my students will come to know (the essential content) or be able to do (the essential skill), and how they will be required to think about that content (essential reasoning processes) as a result of today's lesson.				
• I can describe exactly why I am asking my students to learn this chunk of information *on this day* and *in this way*.				

Which of the following statements describes how you met this target in today's lesson?

☐ I defined a specific learning target for today's lesson—a statement of exactly what my students would be able to do or come to know as a result of today's lesson.

☐ I had a general learning target for today's lesson—a learning statement that was general and covered more than one lesson.

☐ I had an instructional objective for today's lesson. I worked toward an instructional objective from the textbook or the district curriculum that uses professional instructional language to state the important outcomes for this unit or set of lessons.

☐ I did not have a specific purpose for today's lesson. My students were "doing more of the same." It was a repeat of a previous lesson with no unique outcome intended.

State your specific learning target for the lesson and explain why it describes exactly what you are asking your students to come to know or be able to do in this lesson that is unique. How is it different from what they did or learned yesterday and what they will do or learn tomorrow?

Learning Targets: Helping Students Aim for Understanding in Today's Lesson
Connie M. Moss and Susan M. Brookhart [© 2012 by ASCD. All rights reserved.]

Target 2: Each lesson I teach includes a strong performance of understanding that deepens my students' understanding of the essential content, helps them aim for understanding, allows them to assess their work as they are learning, and enables us to gather evidence of student achievement of the learning target.

I will know I have reached this target when I am able to say . . .	Not Confident	Not Very Confident	Somewhat Confident	Very Confident
• I can require that what my students actually do, say, write, or make during today's lesson will produce compelling evidence of what they understand and/or are able to do in relation to the learning target.				

Which of the following statements describes what you required your students to actually do, say, make, or write during today's lesson? Below the statement you select, describe the activity.

☐ My students engaged in a strong performance of understanding. My students engaged in a learning experience during today's lesson that deepened their understanding of the learning target's essential content and skills, required them to use reasoning processes, promoted self-assessment, and produced compelling evidence of where they are in relation to the specific learning target for today's lesson.

☐ My students engaged in a learning activity. I asked students to engage in an activity that was related to the learning target and produced general evidence of what they know and are able to do or evidence of what some of them know or are able to do.

☐ What I asked my students to do during the lesson did not produce evidence of where they are in relation to the learning target. The activity was unrelated or minimally related to the learning target or produced little to no evidence of what students know or can do in relation to the learning target.

☐ I did not require my students to actually do something with the content or the skills that were the focus of my lesson.

Describe exactly what you required students to do during the lesson. What was the task? How long did it take? What did students produce that you could assess? What did they do that you could observe and assess? What evidence would students glean about what they knew well, knew some of, or did not know to help them self-assess and self-regulate?

Target 3: My students and I gather strong evidence of learning using specific success criteria and student look-fors that reveal where students are in relation to the learning target for today's lesson.

I will know I have reached this target when I am able to say . . .	Not Confident	Not Very Confident	Somewhat Confident	Very Confident
• I can describe exactly what I will "look for" to support my claim that my students have mastered the learning target for today's lesson.				
• I can describe the specific characteristics of quality work that I will use to assess what my students did to demonstrate mastery of the essential content and skills that are part of the learning target for today's lesson.				
• I can describe and explain what success looks like for today's lesson so that my students are able to assess their mastery of the essential knowledge and skills that are central to the learning target for today's lesson.				

Which of the following statements describes how you and your students assessed student success in today's lesson?

☐ My students and I assessed the quality of my students' work and performance using specific success criteria for the learning target in today's lesson.

☐ I did not share the criteria for success for today's lesson with my students. I was the only one able to assess the quality of their work and performance using specific success criteria for the learning target in today's lesson.

☐ I did not have specific success criteria that described what good work in the lesson would look like so that my students and I could gauge where we were in relation to the learning target. Instead, I ranked the students' performance using letter grades, scores, percentages, or number correct.

☐ I had no standard of quality for what my students did to demonstrate mastery of the learning target in today's lesson.

☐ I did not require my students to actually do something during today's lesson that I could observe or assess to gauge what they understood or could do in relation to the learning target.

Describe exactly what you used to assess the students' level of understanding or skill as you proceeded with the lesson. And describe exactly what your students used to assess the quality of the work they produced during this lesson to demonstrate mastery of the lesson's essential content or skill(s).

Target 4: In each of my lessons I use multiple strategies along with a performance of understanding to share the learning target with my students.

I will know I have reached this target when I am able to say . . .	Not Confident	Not Very Confident	Somewhat Confident	Very Confident
• I can use multiple ways to weave the learning target into the fabric of today's lesson so that my students can see, understand, and use it throughout the formative learning cycle to improve their learning and achievement.				

Which of the remaining statements below (at least two, but check all that apply) describe how you shared the learning target for today's lesson with your students so that they understood and actively used it to plan and assess their work? Support each statement you select with specific evidence of what you did during today's lesson. Notice that the first statement has been checked for you. Without a performance of understanding, students have no chance to aim for understanding.

☑ I required a strong performance of understanding of my students because it is the single best way to share the learning target and success criteria with them.

Describe exactly what you required your students to do to produce evidence of their mastery of the learning target for today's lesson.

☐ I verbally shared the target.

Describe exactly what you said and when and how you said it.

☐ I asked students to paraphrase the target, put it into their own words, or explain the target to a friend to make sure they understood exactly where they were headed in today's lesson.

☐ I used a visual (picture, chart, SMART Board, or student handout) to help my students see, recognize, and understand the specific learning target for today's lesson.

Describe the visual and why it was specific to today's lesson. How did you use the visual? Describe exactly what you and the students did with it.

☐ I referred to the learning target throughout the lesson, helping students gauge where they were in relation to the learning target.

How, specifically, did you do this, and why?

☐ I shared examples of strong and weak work and gave students the chance to examine the characteristics of each to better understand what success would look like for today's lesson.

What did the examples look like, and where did you get them? Did you create them? Were they anonymous samples from previous students? How did the students use the examples? In groups? With a rubric?

☐ I connected what students were learning and doing in today's lesson to what they would be asked to do in the lesson(s) coming next in this unit and/or to what they learned and did in yesterday's lesson.

What did you say or demonstrate to your students that helped them make the connections between what they already learned, were learning today, and would be learning tomorrow?

Target 5: During each lesson, I consistently feed my students' learning forward toward the learning target.

I will know I have reached this target when I am able to say . . .	Not Confident	Not Very Confident	Somewhat Confident	Very Confident
• I can provide feedback that is directly related to the learning target for today's lesson.				
• I can provide feedback that describes exactly what students did well and not so well in relation to the success criteria.				
• I can describe next-step strategies students should use to improve or learn more.				
• I can provide feedback while my students still have the opportunity to use it.				
• I can provide feedback that uses student-friendly, developmentally appropriate language.				

Which of the following statements describes your actions? Check all that apply. Support each statement you select with specific evidence of what you did during today's lesson.

☐ I consistently provided feedback that was related to the learning target and criteria for success, describing what the student did well and which criteria were not met and why.

☐ I fed students' learning forward during the introductory part of the lesson—I modeled and explained by pointing out what was important to learn and be able to do, and described or demonstrated specific strategies for doing so.

☐ I used the criteria for success to "explain" the concepts in the lesson in ways that helped the students envision what success would look like for the lesson, understand the characteristics of a strong student performance of understanding, and set goals for improving their work.

Learning Targets: Helping Students Aim for Understanding in Today's Lesson
Connie M. Moss and Susan M. Brookhart [© 2012 by ASCD. All rights reserved.]

☐ I referred to the learning target and the success criteria to feed students' learning forward during guided practice.

☐ I pointed out specific strategies related to the learning target that students could use to improve their work as I described what the students would be asked to do during the performance of understanding.

☐ I used written, verbal, or modeling feedback to feed learning forward and close the gaps in understanding or skill that I discovered during the performance of understanding.

☐ I chose the appropriate audience (an individual student, a group of students, or the entire class) to deliver feedback that was targeted to the specific students' needs and strengths.

☐ I delivered feedback that described where the students were in relation to the learning target and suggested next steps for improvement while the students still had time to act on the feedback to improve their work.

☐ I provided enough feedback after the student performance of understanding so that students could be mindful of the assignment criteria for success and know exactly what they should do next to improve their work.

Learning Targets: Helping Students Aim for Understanding in Today's Lesson
Connie M. Moss and Susan M. Brookhart [© 2012 by ASCD. All rights reserved.]

Target 6: During each lesson, I consistently teach my students how to set goals for their learning and assess the quality of their work.

I will know I have reached this target when I am able to say . . .	Not Confident	Not Very Confident	Somewhat Confident	Very Confident
• I used a formative learning cycle during today's lesson to constantly feed my students' learning forward toward challenging learning goals.				
• My students understand the process of self-assessment and used it before, during, and after the performance of understanding in today's lesson.				
• My students can apply the success criteria to set mastery goals for increasing their understanding and producing quality work during today's lesson.				
• My students can accurately apply success criteria to their own work to describe exactly what they know and can do well and exactly where they need to increase their understanding.				
• My students consistently seek feedback and ask questions about how to improve their learning during today's lesson.				

Which of the following statements describes your actions? Check all that apply. Support each statement you select with specific evidence of what you did during today's lesson.

☐ I engaged my students in an appropriate level of challenge that required them to seek clarity and teacher feedback.

☐ I helped my students aim for mastery goals by describing what we would do in today's lesson in terms of their increased understanding and skill.

☐ I wove my feed-forward information throughout the formative learning cycle in today's lesson to encourage student goal setting and self-assessment.

☐ I engaged students in a strong performance of understanding and encouraged them to assess their own progress as they were learning.

☐ I provided timely feedback on the performance of understanding to help my students compare their assessment with my feedback.

☐ I provided a "golden second chance" during today's lesson—the opportunity for my students to use my feedback to improve their performance during an additional task.

Learning Targets: Helping Students Aim for Understanding in Today's Lesson
Connie M. Moss and Susan M. Brookhart [© 2012 by ASCD. All rights reserved.]

ACTION TOOL E:
Student Self-Assessment and Intentional Learning Guide

My Learning Target:			
My Look-Fors	**I need to work on this**	**I am unsure of or confused about this**	**I am already good at this**
I can			
I can			
I can			

Mark where you are on your way to the learning target. → → → → → →

My Goals for Today's Lesson Thinking about what I am already good at, where I am confused, and what I need to work on, here is what I plan to do during today's lesson to aim for and hit my learning target.
1.
2.
3.

My Questions Thinking about the goals I have for improving my understanding and work, here are the questions I have about what I am learning and being asked to do. Getting these questions answered will help me hit my learning target.
1.
2.
3.

My Learning Strategies This is exactly what I can do to improve my learning and do quality work.
1.
2.
3.

ACTION TOOL F:
No More "Garbage In, Garbage Out": Understanding Connections Among Instruction, Assessment, and Grading

Challenge Questions

- If you could freeze-frame a moment during your school day, in what percentage of the classes would you find *students* performing some activity, assignment, or assessment?
- If you could freeze-frame a moment during your school day, what percentage of the activities, assignments, or assessments in which students were engaged would give *direct evidence* about the knowledge and/or skills that students were intended to learn?

Big Ideas

- A performance of understanding engages students directly with intended content and skills (in the process showing them what these mean); deepens their understanding; and provides strong evidence of what they know and can do.
- What students do, make, say, or write gives both the teacher and the student evidence of learning.
- How you *observe* or *score* a performance of understanding defines its value as evidence.
- Performances of understanding promote student goal setting and motivation to learn.
- Every lesson needs a performance of understanding for its particular learning target. Feedback should directly reflect expectations for learning.
- Instructional activities, formative and summative assessments, and grades should reflect coherent and coordinated performances of understanding.
- Graded performance should be a direct match with expectations for learning. Graded performances can match expectations for learning by
  - Summing up a set of lesson-sized performances of understanding.
  - Checking up on cumulative knowledge and skill developed over time (performance of understanding of a unit goal or standard).

Learning Targets: Helping Students Aim for Understanding in Today's Lesson
Connie M. Moss and Susan M. Brookhart [© 2012 by ASCD. All rights reserved.]

The Concept

PERFORMANCE	OF	UNDERSTANDING
What students do, make, say, or write	Shows students' . . . Develops students' . . . Gives evidence of . . .	Essential knowledge and skills that students are intended to learn

Example

PERFORMANCE	OF	UNDERSTANDING
In groups, students make models or diagrams of their chosen planet's rotation and revolution patterns, then individually write paragraphs explaining what that means for their planet.	Shows students' . . . Develops students' . . . Gives evidence of . . .	Movement patterns of planets in our solar system

Counterexample

PERFORMANCE	OF	UNDERSTANDING
In groups, students look up facts about a chosen planet and put these on a "creative" poster.	Shows students' . . . Develops students' . . . Gives evidence of . . .	Movement patterns of planets in our solar system

Learning Targets: Helping Students Aim for Understanding in Today's Lesson
Connie M. Moss and Susan M. Brookhart [© 2012 by ASCD. All rights reserved.]

The Concept

GRADING	OF	LEARNING
Set of graded assessments [Sets of grades based on what students did, made, said, or wrote]	Shows students and others current standing regarding . . .	Essential knowledge and skills that students were intended to learn

Example

GRADING	OF	LEARNING
• Test on planets • Paragraphs explaining planet movements • Report comparing two planets' characteristics and movements	Shows students and others current standing regarding . . .	Characteristics and movement patterns of the planets in our solar system

Counterexample

GRADING	OF	LEARNING
• Group planet posters • Report on telescopes or rockets	~~Shows students and others current standing regarding . . .~~	Characteristics and movement patterns of the planets in our solar system

Learning Targets: Helping Students Aim for Understanding in Today's Lesson
Connie M. Moss and Susan M. Brookhart

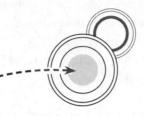

GLOSSARY

ASSESSMENT-CAPABLE STUDENTS: Students who (a) understand and aim for the learning target for today's lesson and (b) know the success criteria and can self-assess accurately against the criteria. Because they understand the learning target, assessment-capable students also understand their next steps in learning and are able to set mastery goals and monitor their progress. Because they are skilled at using success criteria, assessment-capable students can also peer-assess.

CLASSROOM LEARNING TEAM: A learning partnership between the teacher and the students. Each half of the team takes equal responsibility to aim for and assess progress toward the learning target.

DIFFERENTIATED INSTRUCTION: Instruction that matches the needs of students with the requirements for achievement. Differentiated instruction is characterized by using multiple, flexible approaches to learning targets for students at varying levels of readiness and with different interests and attitudes toward the targets.

FEEDBACK THAT FEEDS FORWARD: Student-friendly, developmentally appropriate language that compares student work with the learning target, describes what the student did well in terms of the success criteria and what the student should do next to improve, and suggests a specific strategy for doing it. The information arrives during the performance of understanding or as close to it as possible so that the student can use it to improve his or her work.

FORMATIVE ASSESSMENT: "An active and intentional learning process that partners the teacher and the students to continuously and systematically gather evidence of learning with the express goal of improving student achievement" (Moss & Brookhart, 2009, p. 6).

FORMATIVE LEARNING CYCLE: A five-phase learning cycle focused by a learning target and success criteria. During a formative learning cycle, teachers (1) use feedforward strategies to model and explain the learning intention for today's lesson; (2) scaffold student understanding during guided practice; (3) provide cognitive coaching during a performance of understanding; (4) give detailed, descriptive feedback on the performance; and (5) provide students with the golden opportunity to immediately use that feedback to improve their work.

GRADING: Summing up student achievement for either one assessment or a reporting period. Grades usually take the form of a score, a letter, or a proficiency-level designation. Sometimes called *marking*.

LEARNING TARGET: A description of what the student is going to learn by the end of today's lesson, stated in developmentally appropriate language that the student can understand. Learning target language is framed from the point of view of a student who has not yet mastered the target and includes student look-fors—criteria that students can use to judge how close they are to the target—stated in language that describes mastery (rather than grading or scoring). The learning target is connected to the specific performance of understanding for today's lesson.

MEANINGFUL LEARNING: The acquisition of knowledge and skills at a deep enough level that the student can use them to solve problems, develop further ideas, create original connections, evaluate the importance or worth of an idea or solution, and engage in other applications of higher-order thinking. Sometimes referred to as *teaching for transfer*.

PERFORMANCE OF UNDERSTANDING: A learning experience or task during today's lesson that requires students to aim for the learning target, apply the success criteria, deepen their understanding, and produce compelling evidence of what they know and can do with regard to the learning target.

POTENTIAL LEARNING TRAJECTORY: A goal-directed and appropriately challenging developmental learning path that builds on what students learned in previous lessons, prepares them for the increased challenge in tomorrow's lesson, and leads to significant long-range learning outcomes.

STUDENT LOOK-FORS: A student-friendly term that teachers use to mean *success criteria*. The term is stated in feed-forward language that helps set students up to use the criteria for self-assessment, self-regulation, and goal setting.

STUDENT SELF-EFFICACY: A student's belief that he or she is capable of succeeding in a specific situation or task. A student's sense of self-efficacy plays a major role in how the student approaches goals, tasks, and challenges.

STUDENT SELF-REGULATION: Cognitive, metacognitive, affective, and behavioral processes that a student uses intentionally and systematically to set and attain personal goals for learning.

SUCCESS CRITERIA: Descriptions of what it means to do quality work in today's lesson in terms that are lesson-sized, observable, and measurable, so that students can use them to assess the quality of their work while they are learning. Success criteria are specific to the learning target, understandable, and public.

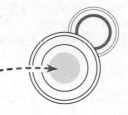

REFERENCES

Ames, C., & Archer, J. (1988). Achievement goals in the classroom: Students' learning strategies and motivation processes. *Journal of Educational Psychology, 80,* 260–267.

Anderson, L. W., & Krathwohl, D. R. (Eds.). (2001). *A taxonomy for learning, teaching, and assessing: A revision of Bloom's Taxonomy of Educational Objectives* (Complete edition). New York: Longman.

Andrade, H. L., Du, Y., & Mycek, K. (2010). Rubric-referenced self-assessment and middle school students' writing. *Assessment in Education, 17*(2), 199–214.

Andrade, H. L., Du, Y., & Wang, X. (2008). Putting rubrics to the test: The effect of a model, criteria generation, and rubric-referenced self-assessment on elementary students' writing. *Educational Measurement: Issues and Practice, 27*(2), 3–13.

Argyris, C., & Schön, D. (1974). *Theory in practice: Increasing professional effectiveness.* San Francisco: Jossey-Bass.

Argyris, C., & Schön, D. (1978) *Organizational learning: A theory of action perspective.* Reading, MA: Addison Wesley.

Asante, M. K., Jr. (2008). *It's bigger than hip-hop: The rise of the post hip-hop generation*. New York: St. Martin's Press.

Atkin, J. M., Black, P., & Coffey, J. (2001). *Classroom assessment and the National Education Standards*. Washington, DC: National Academy Press.

Augustine, C. H., Gonzalez, G., Ikemoto, G. S., Russel, J., Zellman, G. L., Constant, L., Armstrong, J., & Dembosky, J. W. (2009). *Improving school leadership: The promise of cohesive leadership systems* (Commissioned by the Wallace Foundation). Santa Monica, CA: The RAND Corporation.

Bandura, A. (1997). *Self-efficacy: The exercise of control*. New York: W. H. Freeman.

Bandura, A. (2008). Toward an agentic theory of the self. In H. W. Marsh, R. G. Craven, & D. M. Mcinerney (Eds.), *Self-process, learning and enabling human potential* (pp. 15–49). Charlotte, NC: Information Age.

Bandura, A., & Schunk, D. H. (1981). Cultivating competence, self-efficacy, and intrinsic motivation through proximal self-motivation. *Journal of Personality and Social Psychology, 41*(3), 568–598.

Bellon, J., Bellon, E., & Blank, M. A. (1992). *Teaching from a research knowledge base: A development and renewal process*. New York: Macmillan Publishing Company.

Berk, L. E. (2003). *Child development*. Boston: Allyn and Bacon.

Black, P., Harrison, C., Lee, C., Marshall, B., & Wiliam, D. (2002). *Working inside the black box: Assessment for learning in the classroom*. London: King's College London, Department of Education and Professional Studies.

Black, P., & Wiliam, D. (1998). Inside the black box: Raising standards through classroom assessment. *Phi Delta Kappan, 80*(2), 139–148.

Bloom, B. S. (1984). The search for methods of group instruction as effective as one-to-one tutoring. *Educational Leadership, 41*(8), 4–17.

Boekaerts, M. (1999). Self-regulated learning: Where we are today. *International Journal of Educational Research, 31,* 445–457.

Bransford, J. D., & Stein, B. S. (1984). *The IDEAL problem solver*. New York: W. H. Freeman.

Brookhart, S. M. (2008). *How to give effective feedback to your students*. Alexandria, VA: ASCD.

Brookhart, S. M. (2009). *Grading*. Upper Saddle River, NJ: Pearson Education.

Brookhart, S. M. (2010a). *Formative assessment strategies for every classroom: An ASCD Action Tool* (2nd ed.). Alexandria, VA: ASCD.

Brookhart, S. M. (2010b). *How to assess higher-order thinking skills in your classroom*. Alexandria, VA: ASCD.

Brookhart, S. M. (2011). *Grading and learning: Practices that support student achievement.* Bloomington, IN: Solution Tree.

Brookhart, S. M., Andolina, M., Zusa, M., & Furman, R. (2004). Minute math: An action research study of student self-assessment. *Educational Studies in Mathematics, 57*(2), 213–227.

Brookhart, S. M., Moss, C. M., & Long, B. A. (2009). Promoting student ownership of learning through high-impact formative assessment practices. *Journal of Multi-Disciplinary Evaluation, 6*(12), 52–67. Available: http://survey.ate.wmich.edu/jmde/index.php/jmde_1/article/view/234/229

Brookhart, S. M., Moss, C. M., & Long, B. A. (2010). Teacher inquiry into formative assessment practices in remedial reading classrooms. *Assessment in Education, 17*(1), 41–58.

Brookhart, S. M., Moss, C. M., & Long, B. A. (2011). *Principals' and supervisors' roles in helping teachers use formative assessment information.* Paper presented at the annual meeting of the American Educational Research Association, New Orleans, LA.

Brophy, J. (2004). *Motivating students to learn* (2nd ed.). Mahwah, NJ: Erlbaum.

Brown, W. (2008). Young children assess their learning: The power of the quick check strategy. *Young Children, 63*(6), 14–20.

Camburn, E., Rowan, B., & Taylor, J. E. (2003). Distributed leadership in schools: The case of elementary schools adopting comprehensive school reform models. *Educational Evaluation and Policy Analysis, 25*(4), 347–373.

Chappuis, S., & Chappuis, J. (2008). The best value in formative assessment. *Educational Leadership, 65*(4), 14–18.

Chemers, M. M., Watson, C. B., & May, S. (2000). Dispositional affect and leadership effectiveness: A comparison of self-esteem, optimism and efficacy. *Personality and Social Psychology Bulletin, 26,* 267–277.

City, E. A., Elmore, R. F., Fiarman, S. E., & Teitel, L. (2009). *Instructional rounds in education: A network approach to improving teaching.* Cambridge, MA: Harvard Education Press.

Clarke, S. (2001). *Unlocking formative assessment: Practical strategies for enhancing pupils' learning in the primary classroom.* London: Hodder & Stoughton.

Common Core State Standards Initiative. (2010). *Common standards.* Available: http://www.corestandards.org

Cornoldi, C. (2010). Metacognition, intelligence, and academic performance. In H. S. Waters & W. Schneider (Eds.), *Metacognition, strategy use and instruction* (pp. 257–277). New York: Guilford Press.

Darling-Hammond, L., Barron, B., Pearson, P. D., Schoenfeld, A. H., Stage, E. K., Zimmerman, T. D., Cervetti, G. N., & Tilson, J. L. (2008). *Powerful learning: What we know about teaching for understanding.* San Francisco: Jossey-Bass.

Darling-Hammond, L., LaPointe, M., Meyerson, D., Orr, M. T., & Cohen, C. (2007). *Preparing school leaders for a changing world: Lessons from exemplary leadership development programs.* Stanford, CA: Stanford Educational Leadership Institute, Stanford University.

Dewey, J. (1900). *School and society.* Chicago: University of Chicago Press.

Dignath, C., & Büttner, G. (2008). Components of fostering self-regulated learning among students: A meta-analysis on intervention studies at primary and secondary school level. *Metacognition and Learning, 3*(3), 231–264.

Doyle, W., & Rutherford, B. (1984). Classroom research on matching learning and teaching styles. *Theory into Practice, 23*(1), 20–25.

Dweck, C. S. (2000). *Self-theories: Their role in motivation, personality and development.* Lillington, NC: Taylor & Francis.

Educational Testing Service. (2009). *Research rationale for the Keeping Learning on Track program.* Retrieved June 25, 2010, from http://www.ets.org/Media/Campaign/12652/rsc/pdf/KLT-Resource-Rationale.pdf

Facione, P. (2010). *Critical thinking: What it is and why it counts.* Millbrae, CA: Measured Reasons and the California Academic Press. Available: http://www.insightassessment.com/pdf_files/what&why2009.pdf

Grimes, K. J., & Stevens, D. D. (2009). Glass, bug, mud. *Phi Delta Kappan, 90*(9), 677–680.

Guskey, T. R. (2007). Formative classroom assessment and Benjamin S. Bloom: Theory, research, and practice. In J. H. McMillan (Ed.), *Formative classroom assessment: Theory into practice* (pp. 63–78). New York: Teachers College Press.

Hall, T., Strangman, N., & Meyer, A. (2011, January). *Differentiated instruction and implications for UDL implementation.* Wakefield, MA: National Center on Accessing the General Curriculum. Available: http://aim.cast.org/learn/historyarchive/backgroundpapers/differentiated_instruction_udl

Hallinger, P. (2005). Instructional leadership and the school principal: A passing fancy that refuses to fade away. *Leadership and Policy in Schools, 4,* 1–20.

Halverson, R., Grigg, J., Prichett, R., & Thomas, C. (2007). The new instructional leadership: Creating data-driven instructional systems in school. *Journal of School Leadership, 17*(2).

Hattie, J. A. C. (2002). What are the attributes of excellent teachers? In *Teachers make a difference: What is the research evidence?* (pp. 3–26). Wellington, New Zealand: New Zealand Council for Educational Research.

Hattie, J. (2009). *Visible learning: A synthesis of over 800 meta-analyses relative to achievement*. New York: Routledge.

Hattie, J. (2012). *Visible learning for teachers: Maximizing impact on learning*. New York: Routledge.

Hattie, J., & Timperley, H. (2007). The power of feedback. *Review of Educational Research, 77*(1), 81–112.

Heritage, M. (2010). *Formative assessment: Making it happen in the classroom*. Thousand Oaks, CA: Corwin Press.

Higgins, K. M., Harris, N. A., & Kuehn, L. L. (1994). Placing assessment into the hands of young children: A study of self-generated criteria and self-assessment. *Educational Assessment, 2,* 309–324.

Hoffman, J. V., & Rasinski, T. V. (2003). Theory and research into practice: Oral reading in the school literacy curriculum. *Reading Research Quarterly, 38,* 510–522.

Hyman, R., & Rosoff, B. (1984). Matching learning and teaching styles: The jug and what's in it. *Theory into Practice, 23*(1), 35–43.

James, M., Black, P., Carmichael, P., Conner, C., Dudley, P., Fox, A., et al. (2006). *Learning how to learn: Tools for schools*. London: Routledge.

Johnson, D. W., & Johnson, R. T. (2009). An educational psychology success story: Social interdependence theory and cooperative learning. *Educational Researcher, 38*(5), 365–379.

Johnson, R. B., & Christensen, L. B. (2012). *Educational research: Quantitative, qualitative, and mixed approaches* (4th ed.). Thousand Oaks, CA: SAGE Publications.

Kagan, S. (1989/1990). The structural approach to cooperative learning. *Educational Leadership, 47*(4), 12–15.

Katz, L. G. (2009). Where I stand on standardization: A review of *Standardized Childhood. Educational Researcher, 38*(1), 52–53.

Kendall, J. S., & Marzano, R. J. (2004). *Content knowledge: A compendium of standards and benchmarks for K–12 education*. Aurora, CO: Mid-continent Research for Education and Learning. Online database: http://www.mcrel.org/standards-benchmarks

Leighton, J. P. (2011). A cognitive model for the assessment of higher-order thinking in students. In G. Schraw & D. R. Robinson (Eds.), *Assessment of higher-order thinking skills*. Charlotte, NC: Information Age Publishing.

Leithwood, K. A. (2007). Transformation school leadership in a transactional policy world. In *The Jossey-Bass Reader on Educational Leadership* (2nd ed.) (pp. 183–196). San Francisco: Jossey-Bass.

Leithwood, K., Louis, K. S., Anderson, S., & Wahlstrom, K. (2004). *How leadership influences student learning*. Minneapolis, MN: Center for Applied Research and Educational Improvement, University of Minnesota.

Leithwood, K. A., & Riehl, C. (2003). *What we know about successful school leadership*. Philadelphia: Laboratory for Student Success, Temple University.

Locke, E. A., & Latham, G. P. (1990). *A theory of goal-setting and task performance*. Englewood Cliffs, NJ: Prentice-Hall.

Locke, E. A., & Latham, G. P. (2002). Building a practically useful theory of goal setting and task performance. *American Psychologist, 57,* 705–717.

Locke, E. A., & Latham, G. P. (2006). New directions in goal-setting theory. *Current Directions in Psychological Science, 15*(5), 265–268.

Louis, K. S., Leithwood, K., Wahlstrom, K. L., & Anderson, S. E. (2010). *Learning from leadership: Investigating the links to improved student learning*. Final report of research to the Wallace Foundation. Minneapolis, MN: University of Minnesota Center for Applied Research and Educational Improvement.

McCormick, M. J. (2001). Self-efficacy and leadership effectiveness: Applying social cognitive theory to leadership. *Journal of Leadership Studies, 8*(1), 23–33.

Montalvo, F. T., & Gonzales Torres, M. C. (2004). Self-regulated learning: Current and future directions. *Electronic Journal of Research in Educational Psychology, 2*(1), 1–34. Available: http://www.investigacion-psicopedagogica.org/revista/new/english/ContadorArticulo.php?27

Mosenthal, J., Lipson, M., Torncello, S., Russ, B., & Mekkelson, J. (2004). Contexts and practices of six schools successful in obtaining reading achievement. *Elementary School Journal, 104*(5), 343–367.

Moss, C. M. (2002, April). *In the eye of the beholder: The role of educational psychology in teacher inquiry.* Paper presented at the annual meeting of the American Educational Research Association, New Orleans, LA.

Moss, C. M., & Brookhart, S. M. (2009). *Advancing formative assessment in every classroom: A guide for instructional leaders*. Alexandria, VA: ASCD.

Moss, C. M., Brookhart, S. M., & Long, B. A. (2011a). *School administrators' formative assessment leadership practices*. Paper presented at the annual meeting of the American Educational Research Association, New Orleans, LA.

Moss, C. M., Brookhart, S. M., & Long, B. A. (2011b). *What are the students actually doing? Preparing principals who gather strong evidence of learning*. Paper presented at the annual meeting of the University Council for Educational Administration, Pittsburgh, PA.

Moss, C. M., Brookhart, S. M., & Long, B. A. (2011c). Knowing your learning target. *Educational Leadership, 68*(6), 66–69.

National College for School Leadership (NCSL). (2007). *What we know about school leadership*. Nottingham, UK: Author. Available: http://www.nationalcollege.org.uk/docinfo?id=17480&!lename=what-we-know-about-schoolleadership.pdf

National Conference of State Legislatures. (2002). *The role of school leadership in improving student achievement*. Washington, DC: Author. (ERIC Document Reproduction Service No. ED479288)

Neill, A. S. (1960). *Summerhill: A radical approach to child-rearing*. New York: Hart Publishing.

Norris, S. P., & Ennis, R. H. (1989). *Evaluating critical thinking*. Pacific Grove, CA: Critical Thinking Press & Software.

O'Connor, K. (2009). *How to grade for learning K–12* (3rd ed.). Thousand Oaks, CA: Corwin Press.

Ormrod, J. E. (2009). *Essentials of educational psychology* (2nd ed.). Upper Saddle River, NJ: Pearson Education.

Ormrod, J. E. (2011a). *Our minds, our memories: Enhancing thinking and learning at all ages*. Boston: Pearson.

Ormrod, J. E. (2011b). *Educational psychology: Developing learners* (7th ed.). Boston: Pearson.

Pajares, F. (2006). Self-efficacy during childhood and adolescence: Implications for teachers and parents. In F. Pajares & T. Urdan (Eds.), *Self-efficacy beliefs of adolescents* (pp. 339–367). Greenwich, CT: Information Age Publishers.

Perkins, D., & Blythe, T. (1994, February). Putting understanding up front. *Educational Leadership, 51*(5), 4–7.

Reeves, D. B. (2004). The case against the zero. *Phi Delta Kappan, 86*(4), 324–325.

Rolheiser, C., Bower, B., & Stevahn, L. (2000). *The portfolio organizer: Succeeding with portfolios in your classroom*. Alexandria, VA: ASCD.

Ross, J. A., Hogaboam-Gray, A., & Rolheiser, C. (2002). Student self-evaluation in grade 5–6 mathematics: Effects on problem-solving achievement. *Educational Assessment, 8*(1), 43–58.

Ross, J. A., & Starling, M. (2008). Self-assessment in a technology-supported environment: The case of grade 9 geography. *Assessment in Education, 15*(2), 183–199.

Sadler, R. (1989). Formative assessment and the design of instructional systems. *Instructional Science, 18,* 119–144.

Sato, M., & Atkin, J. M. (2006/2007). Supporting change in classroom assessment. *Educational Leadership, 64*(4), 76–79.

Schön, D. A. (1983). *The reflective practitioner: How professionals think in action.* London: Temple Smith.

Schreiber, J. B., & Moss, C. M. (2002). A Peircean view of teacher beliefs and genuine doubt. *Teaching and Learning: The Journal of Natural Inquiry and Reflective Practice, 17*(1), 25–42.

Scott, C. (2010). The enduring appeal of "learning styles." *Australian Journal of Education, 54*(1), 5–17.

Silins, H., & Mulford, B. (2004). Schools as learning organizations—Effects on teacher leadership and student outcomes. *School Effectiveness and School Improvement, 15*(3–4), 443–466.

Sloan, P., & Latham, R. (1981). *Teaching reading is . . .* Melbourne, Australia: Nelson.

Small, M. (2010). Beyond one right answer. *Educational Leadership, 68*(1), 29–32.

Spillane, J. P., Hallett, T., & Diamond, J. B. (2003). Forms of capital and the construction of readership: Instructional leadership in urban elementary schools. *Sociology of Education, 76*(1), 1–17.

Tomlinson, C. A. (2001). *How to differentiate instruction in mixed-ability classrooms* (2nd ed.). Alexandria, VA: ASCD.

Tomlinson, C. A. (2003). *Fulfilling the promise of the differentiated classroom: Strategies and tools for responsive teaching.* Alexandria, VA: ASCD.

Vatterott, C. (2009). *Rethinking homework: Best practices that support diverse needs.* Alexandria, VA: ASCD.

Webb, N. L. (2002). *Alignment study in language arts, mathematics, science and social studies of state standards and assessments for four states.* Washington, DC: Council of Chief State School Officers.

Wiliam, D. (2010). An integrative summary of the research literature and implications for a new theory of formative assessment. In H. Andrade & G. Cizek (Eds.), *Handbook of formative assessment* (pp. 18–40). New York: Routledge.

Wormeli, R. (2006). *Fair isn't always equal: Assessing and grading in the differentiated classroom.* Portland, ME: Stenhouse Publishers.

Zaccaro, S. J., Blair, V., Peterson, C., & Zazanis, M. (1995). Collective efficacy. In J. E. Maddux (Ed.), *Self-efficacy, adaptation and adjustment: Theory, research and application.* New York: Plenum.

Zimmerman, B. J. (2001). Theories of self-regulated learning and academic achievement: An overview and analysis. In B. J. Zimmerman & D. H. Schunk (Eds.), *Self-regulated learning and academic achievement: Theoretical perspectives* (pp. 1–65). Mahwah, NJ: Lawrence Erlbaum Associates.

Zimmerman, B. J., Bonner, S., & Kovach, R. (1996). *Developing self-regulated learners: Beyond achievement to self-efficacy.* Washington, DC: American Psychological Association.

Zimmerman, B. J., & Cleary, T. J. (2006). Adolescents' development of personal agency: The role of self-efficacy beliefs and self-regulatory skill. In F. Pajares & T. Urdan (Eds.), *Self-efficacy beliefs of adolescents* (pp. 45–69). Greenwich, CT: Information Age Publishers.

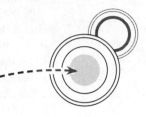

INDEX

Information in figures is denoted by *f*.

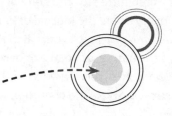

ABOUT THE AUTHORS

Connie M. Moss, EdD, is an associate professor in the Department of Educational Foundations and Leadership in the School of Education at Duquesne University and director of the Center for Advancing the Study of Teaching and Learning (CASTL). She served for 25 years as a K–12 educator, spending 17 of those years in early childhood, elementary, and middle school classrooms. She continued her public school service as an educational leader of multidistrict, regional, and statewide initiatives in curriculum planning and assessment. The recipient of numerous teaching awards, she has been an invited speaker and presenter in over 600 school districts, 100 universities and colleges, and many educational associations and organizations. She is the coauthor, with Susan M. Brookhart, of ASCD's *Advancing Formative Assessment in Every Classroom.* She may be reached at moss@castl.duq.edu.

Susan M. Brookhart, PhD, is an independent educational consultant based in Helena, Montana. She has taught both elementary and middle school. She was professor and chair of the Department of Educational Foundations and Leadership at Duquesne University, where she currently serves as senior research associate in the Center for

Advancing the Study of Teaching and Learning in the School of Education. She serves on the state assessment advisory committee for the state of Montana. She has been the education columnist for *National Forum,* the journal of Phi Kappa Phi, and editor of *Educational Measurement: Issues and Practice,* a journal of the National Council on Measurement in Education. She is the author or coauthor of several books, including ASCD's *How to Give Effective Feedback to Your Students* and *How to Assess Higher-Order Thinking Skills in Your Classroom.* She is the coauthor, with Connie M. Moss, of ASCD's *Advancing Formative Assessment in Every Classroom.* She may be reached at susanbrookhart@bresnan.net.

WHOLE CHILD
TENETS

THE **WHOLE CHILD**

The ASCD Whole Child approach is an effort to transition from a focus on narrowly defined academic achievement to one that promotes the long-term development and success of all children. Through this approach, ASCD supports educators, families, community members, and policymakers as they move from a vision about educating the whole child to sustainable, collaborative actions.

Learning Targets relates to the **engaged**, **supported**, and **challenged** tenets. *For more about the ASCD Whole Child approach, visit **www.ascd.org/wholechild.***

1 HEALTHY
Each student enters school healthy and learns about and practices a healthy lifestyle.

2 SAFE
Each student learns in an environment that is physically and emotionally safe for students and adults.

3 ENGAGED
Each student is actively engaged in learning and is connected to the school and broader community.

4 SUPPORTED
Each student has access to personalized learning and is supported by qualified, caring adults.

5 CHALLENGED
Each student is challenged academically and prepared for success in college or further study and for employment and participation in a global environment.